Malta

Front cover: a *luzzu* fishing boat

Right: on guard at Mdina's main gate

TOP 10 ATTRACTIONS

Mosta's Santa Maria Assunta Church •
Inspired by the Pantheon in Rome *(page 61)*

Mdina • Malta's former capital is full
of atmospheric medieval streets and
Baroque cultural treasures *(page 54)*

Gozo • This green little island
has retained more of its
traditional lifestyle than its
bigger neighbour *(page 68)*

The Blue Grotto • See the
dazzling azure waters of this
lovely sea cave *(page 51)*

St John's Co-Cathedral The severe façade of this Valletta landmark belies the ornate beauty to be found within *(page 30)*

The Citadel in Gozo This impressive fortification was begun by the Arabs *(page 72)*

Marsaxlokk The boats at this picturesque fishing port bear a painted eye to ward off evil *(page 49)*

Mellieħa Bay The best sandy beach on Malta, Għadira, lies on this beautiful bay, and borders a nature reserve *(page 67)*

Watersports The crystal-clear waters around the islands make Malta a popular choice for watersport enthusiasts *(page 87)*

Ancient temples Sites such as the 5400-year-old Mnajdra bear witness to Malta's unique early history *(page 52)*

29

CONTENTS

24

47

45

76

93

INTRODUCTION

The tiny island of Malta sits at the heart of the Mediterranean Sea. Although only 316 sq km (122 sq miles) in area, its land has felt the ebb and flow of the most influential ancient cultures, and its people have witnessed at first hand pivotal moments in European history. Settled as early as 5200BC and coveted throughout its long history by the dominant power brokers of every age, Malta's amazing natural harbours have offered safety for some and contributed to disaster for others.

Six islands comprise the archipelago of Malta but only three are inhabited. Malta, the largest, is home to more than 400,000 people, while Gozo (known locally as Ghawdex) has one-fifth of this population on an island a quarter of the size. Comino has a hotel and only a handful of houses with no motorised vehicles, and the two St Paul's Bay islands see only day visitors. Finally, there is tiny Filfla, which witnesses only the footsteps of birds and lizards – it is a nature reserve, and no human visitors are allowed.

Location and Landscape

Malta is the most southerly European country, situated approximately halfway between the western and eastern ends of the Mediterranean, and roughly equidistant from the shores of Sicily and North Africa. It is believed to have been attached to Sicily until the end of the last Ice Age, when sea levels rose and washed in to part the islands.

Geologically, the islands are made up of layers of sandstone and limestone – a porous structure that has been eroded over the millennia by the power of wind and water.

Fishing boats at Marsaxlokk

Hundreds of narrow coves have been cut into the coastline, interspersed with high cliffs and a few sandy bays. Ancient watercourses once flowed across the Maltese landscape, and these supported populations of dwarf hippopotamuses and elephants; hundreds of fossilised skeletons have been found in the cave of Għar Dalam in the south of Malta. Today the rivers have dried up, so Malta relies on winter rainfall, as well as a technologically advanced desalinisation process for its water supply.

In spring, the island's cliffs and rural waysides are awash with wild grasses and a plethora of attractive flowers. During the dry summer months, the hillsides grow parched and brown; the air is hot and still, and only the constant, loud chirping sound of the cicada (the Mediterranean's ubiquitous noisy insect) breaks the silence.

Harbour or honey?

The origin of Malta's name has long been debated. One theory is that it is a corruption of the Phoenician word *malat* ('safe harbour'), although for centuries the island was known as Melita, which is believed to be derived from the Greek *meli* (the word for 'honey'), a famous product of the islands in early times. Gozo (or Għawdex to the locals, pronounced 'Ow-desh') is probably derived from the Greek *gaudos*, which in turn derives from the Phoenician word for a small boat.

Rich Heritage

Settlers probably arrived here from Sicily as early as 5300BC. They were a farming people, independent and self-sufficient. However, as soon as seafaring allowed greater mobility, Malta became an important port on the developing shipping routes, and this began a long tradition of control from abroad by the dominant maritime power in the Mediterranean of each successive era. Over the centuries, Malta was visited or settled by Phoenicians, the

Ancient Greeks, Romans and Arabs. In the 16th century the Emperor Charles V gave Malta to the Order of St John, a military order of Knights Hospitallers, who had attempted unsuccessfully to defend Jerusalem against the Ottoman Turks. Under their dominion, Malta became arguably the world's most fortified place. Their capital, Valletta, is now considered to be a masterpiece of late Medieval and Baroque architecture. In 1798 Napoleon Bonaparte evicted the Knights from their fortifications, but just two years later the French in turn yielded to the British, who then ruled the islands – with some limited self-determination for its inhabitants – until 1964, when Malta gained independence. The islands were declared a republic in 1974 and became part of the European Union on 1 May 2004.

Couvre Porte gate, Vittoriosa

People

And what of the people who have lived so many centuries under the rule of foreign powers? They are some of the most welcoming people you could ever hope to meet. In AD60 when St Paul arrived unexpectedly on the island as the result of a shipwreck off present-day St Paul's Bay, he received as warm a welcome from the people as visitors do today. If you study your map while sightseeing, you are sure to be approached by someone offering to help you with directions, or suggestions about which places to visit.

Throughout the years, the Maltese have remained faithful to their own traditions and have a unique language and culture. Most of the local people speak Malti, the national language which is closely related to Arabic. However, they also have English as a second official language, and Italian and French are widely spoken as well. Therefore, communication is never a problem when you are travelling around the islands.

The Maltese and Gozitans (the people of Gozo) have a fierce loyalty to what they hold dear. Their Catholic faith is an anchor in their lives, and the pride of every village or town is its large, highly decorated parish church. Family relationships are close, and everyone displays a respect for the older members of society.

Perhaps greatest of all is a love of their island, for which the Maltese fought so bravely during World War II that in 1942 Great Britain awarded them its highest award for civil bravery, the George Cross. They are proud of their independence, having one of the highest electoral turnouts in the world. More than 95 percent of the eligible population exercise their right

Festas

Each settlement in the Maltese islands has its own saint's day or *festa*, usually over a weekend. The *festa* commences on a Saturday with a religious parade in which an effigy of the saint is carried through the streets following a band. The community then takes part in a service held at the parish church. The *festa* is not only a religious ritual. It also involves the participation of that most cherished of Maltese institutions, the local brass band, and there are huge firework displays, too. The streets are decorated and stalls sell drinks and refreshments. Visitors are always very welcome to take part.

to vote in elections, and they are vociferous in their opinions on the best way forward for their country.

The Maltese, of course, don't spend all their time in such serious and earnest pursuits: they very much enjoy their relaxed island lifestyle. Whether it is a fisherman mending his nets or keeping his *luzzu* boat spic-and-span, or the waiter calmly going about his business at the harbourside restaurant, there is an unhurried air that helps the visitor to relax too.

A *festa* in full swing

Everyone knows everyone else and there's still a comforting network of mutual support here. A favourite pastime is to stroll along seaside promenades or along Republic Street in Valletta taking in the cool evening air. If there's a new baby to show off, you'll find both grandmothers proudly pushing the pram, basking in the warm congratulations of their neighbours. On Sundays whole families get together for a picnic or long lunch. After eating, the children play noisily while the adults sit around the table discussing the topics of the day.

Changes and Tourism

Although tradition still plays an important part in daily life, Malta has experienced a great deal of change since independence. Tourism has become the focus of wealth creation at a time of major population growth. As well as providing accommodation for locals and visitors, the resulting building

Typical enclosed balconies, the *gallarija*, in Valletta

boom has also put pressure on farmland and fishing communities. Much of the new construction has not been of the most tasteful variety, and a preponderance of concrete blights most of Malta's resorts – although Gozo has made the smarter decision, opting to carry on building in traditional sandstone.

The islands also have so much history – it's woven into the fabric of almost every Maltese building – that the accompanying responsibility can be quite problematic. But restoration plans for neglected historical sites and buildings are in hand and the islands' rich heritage is gradually returning to its former glory. As they are restored, so they open to visitors. For anyone not planning to spend every day seeking sun and sand, there will be even more to do.

Malta is a popular holiday destination. There are warm, clear waters for swimming, snorkelling and diving; footpaths and farm tracks for exploring; and guaranteed hot sunshine between May and October. The islands have many loyal devotees who take a holiday here year after year. They return because, although it has touches of the exotic, Malta has much that feels safe, familiar and comfortable. They also know that they are guaranteed the welcome reserved for a friend, the welcome that the Maltese extend to all their visitors.

A BRIEF HISTORY

Situated at the heart of the Mediterranean Sea, Malta has long been seen by power brokers as an important island. It has played a key role in many of the world's major power struggles and has often been at the centre of key events in the history of Europe.

Civilisation dawned on the islands long before recorded history and the islands are rich in sites to explore. Settlers arrived on Malta during the Neolithic Age, around 5300BC, well after the end of the last Ice Age raised sea levels and separated the island from Sicily. They were farmers and brought wheat and a range of domestic animals with them. Archaeologists think that it was during this first wave of settlement that Malta lost all of its native forest.

It took almost another millennium for any great cultural development to take place, yet when it did, Malta saw the flowering of a sophisticated society, with a high level of building skills and complex rituals surrounding burial of the dead. From 4100BC, a thousand years before the earliest pyramids were built in Egypt, the first settlers began to construct towering free-standing stone temples, including Ġgantija on Gozo and Ħaġar Qim on Malta. The structures probably had wooden roofs and are called temples today because it is thought that religious ceremonies took place inside them. Even the underground

Female fertility figure in the Archaeology Museum

The impressively located Mnajdra temple near Żurrieq

Hypogeum at Paola, where bones from more than 7,000 bodies were discovered in the burial chambers, has an oracle chamber that would have had a priestess present. The Temple Period lasted until 2500BC and its temples are now designated UNESCO World Heritage Sites.

   During the Bronze Age (2500–700BC), small settlements began to take shape. They remained undisturbed until the islands' harbours started to be used by the Phoenician traders in the late 8th century BC and island life began to change.

Carthage and Rome

The Phoenicians were great warriors as well as traders. From their base on the coast of Syria they travelled the Mediterranean and in time established a colony at Carthage in North Africa, which grew into a great trading republic, dominating the whole region. Inscriptions, coins and tombs remain as a record of Phoenician control of Malta from 700 to 500BC.

When a new power, Rome, began to expand southwards, a clash with Carthage was inevitable. Three wars were waged (the Punic Wars) between 264 and 146BC until the Carthaginians were finally defeated. But by then Malta was already in the hands of Rome, having been taken in 218BC by a Roman expeditionary force. The Romans took over Mdina, fortifying it and building luxurious villas on the surrounding high ground. You can see the remains of a Roman house, the Domus Romana, in Rabat, outside Mdina.

Arabs and Crusaders

As the Roman Empire went into decline, it was divided into western and eastern sections. Malta was allocated to the east, governed from Constantinople. It became an important naval base. However, as Roman power declined, Arab influence grew, and after invading the islands in AD870, the Arabs became the new rulers. One of their first actions was to build a fortified citadel at Mdina.

Although the Arab rulers tolerated Christianity, many islanders emigrated, and some remaining Maltese converted to Islam. Two centuries of Arab rule left an indelible impression on Malta and especially on the language. Cotton

St Paul's Shipwreck

In AD60, one of Malta's most important historical events occurred. St Paul and St Luke were shipwrecked just off the island, somewhere in the area now known as St Paul's Bay. They had been travelling from Caesarea for trial in Rome, where Paul was to appeal to Caesar for clemency.

Paul spent the winter months in a cave at Rabat, where he preached Christianity, and his message began the conversion of the islanders. One of the first converts was the 'headman' of Malta living in Mdina, Publius, who was eventually named the island's first bishop.

and citrus fruits were introduced and became the mainstay of the economy as trade expanded.

In 1090 Count Roger II the Norman (they were known as Siculo-Normans) invaded the island from Sicily, but was fought off. However, in 1127 his son, King Roger, succeeded in reconquering the islands and made them part of the Christian Kingdom of Sicily.

Malta was a key link in the line of communication during the Crusades, while passing first through German and French hands before being taken by the Aragonese in 1282 and coming under Spanish rule. It was at this time that the Maltese nobility began to develop. In 1397 a system of local government called the Università was established and several local families became fundamental in its development.

The Knights of St John

The 16th century saw the Mediterranean Sea becoming increasingly dominated by the Ottoman Turks, led by Sultan Suleiman the Magnificent. Their chief adversaries, the crusading Knights of the Order of St John, had long since been expelled from the Holy Land, yet still held on to a base on the island of Rhodes off the coast of Turkey. After repeated attacks and a six-month siege in 1522, the Turks took Rhodes on New Year's Day 1523. Surprisingly, Suleiman was merciful and granted the Knights leave to go. While they were adrift again, they departed with their wealth intact. Philippe Villiers de l'Isle Adam, the courageous Grand Master of the Order,

St John's Cathedral detail

led his soldiers from their home to Sicily and to Italy, where for eight years they were without a base. Eventually, the Holy Roman Emperor, Charles V, offered the island of Malta to them, and in 1530 the Grand Master and his 4,000 men moved to this new base. At that time the islands had around 12,000 inhabitants.

The Order of St John

The story of the Order of St John of Jerusalem (the Knights Hospitallers) begins in the 11th century, when Italian merchants obtained permission from the Muslim caliph to set up a Christian hospice in Jerusalem. The calling of the Order was principally to care for the sick, but in time the emphasis shifted to a military role, that of fighting for the faith. In 1187 the Knights were driven from Jerusalem by Saladin, and spent the following centuries fighting different Muslim leaders from their bases in Acre, Cyprus and Rhodes, before coming to Malta when they were given the islands by Emperor Charles V.

The Knights took vows of poverty, chastity and obedience. They were grouped in eight *langues*, or 'tongues', three of them French (France being divided in the 13th century into France, Provence and Auvergne). The other *langues* were Aragon, Castile, Italy, Germany, and England. In Valletta, each *langue* built an *auberge*, where they lived together. Each *langue* was headed by a *pilier*, who had a set function: thus the *pilier* of Italy was Grand Admiral; the *pilier* of Provence was finance and ordnance manager; the *pilier* of France was head of the order's hospitals. Their head, the Grand Master, was elected for life and was subject only to the authority of the Pope.

As the years passed, corruption and internal dissension undermined the effectiveness and reputation of the Order. However, their place in history and their bravery in war has ensured their fame and honorary title: the Knights of Malta. With headquarters in Rome, the organisation today is known as the Sovereign Military Order of Malta.

The Knights built fortifications and living quarters in the great harbour at Birgu (later called Vittoriosa) and the neighbouring peninsula, Senglea. As the Grand Harbour area became the focus of activity, so the importance of the old capital, Mdina, declined. When the Spanish Inquisition arrived on the island in 1561, the Inquisitor's Palace was built in Birgu.

The Knights had not seen the last of the Turks, however. Suleiman regretted his charitable act and, soon after the Knights arrived in Malta, was plotting to take over the island because of its strategic position. Suleiman considered the Order of St John his old enemy and the islands his stepping-stone to the invasion of mainland Europe. The Knights also found themselves threatened by privateers from north Africa, under the command of one Dragut. They devastated Gozo in 1546 and took thousands of Gozitans as slaves in 1551. And then Dragut joined forces with the rampaging Turks.

The Great Siege

In 1565, when word reached Grand Master La Valette of a huge force approaching his islands, he sent out desperate appeals for help. Only a small number of volunteers came. On 19 May, a Turkish fleet of 181 galleys disembarked an army of 30,000 at Marsaxlokk Bay. Among them were 4,000 fanatical janissaries, mostly converts to Islam, the crack troops of their time. The invaders, with the navy commanded by Admiral Piali and the army by Mustapha Pasha, were confident of victory. La

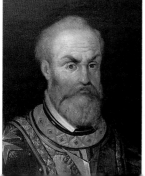

Grand Master Jean Parisot de La Valette

Valette had only his 600 knights, 1,200 infantrymen and a militia of about 5,000 untrained men and slaves as well as eight galleys. These men were to prove astoundingly resilient, as they performed one of the most valiant defences in history.

Throughout the summer of 1565, heat, disease and diminishing food supplies plagued both sides as they battled on. The Maltese people fought and suffered along with the Knights in fierce resistance. Each man lost was irreplaceable, and strategic positions were abandoned one by one for lack of troops to hold them. At one critical

The Siege in progress

point, La Valette himself, although he was aged 72, threw himself into the fray, inspiring his followers by his courage. The valiant defenders gradually wore down the Turks, despite their advantage. Arguments between the two Turk commanders did not help. In one assault alone on Senglea, the Turks lost 2,500 men.

At last, a relief force from the viceroy of Sicily came to the rescue. On 7 September, under Don Garcia de Toledo, they landed at Mellieha Bay. The Turks were fooled into believing the fresh troops to be more numerous than they really were, and they therefore abandoned the siege. As the remnant of the Turkish forces sailed away, their defeat marked the turning point in Ottoman fortunes, and their empire began a slow decline. In Malta there was great rejoicing, although the island was devastated by the siege.

Money poured in from grateful Christian monarchs around Europe, relieved to have been saved from the threat of further Muslim expansion. Plans were drawn up for a new city across the harbour facing Birgu, on the Sceberras peninsula that separates the island's two great harbours. This position could be more easily defended in any future conflict. The Order obtained the services of the Pope's own architect, Francesco Laparelli. The capital was to be called Valletta – named after the resolute Grand Master La Valette (the double L comes from the Italian version of his name). Its modern, grid design allowed for easy movement and cooling breezes, something lacking in the design of medieval Birgu. The plan of the city inspired Maltese architect Gerolamo Cassar. He is responsible for much of the way Valletta looks today, with fine, harmonious buildings blending early Baroque with classical elements.

The Auberge de Castille

By the 18th century, however, much of the Mediterranean was in the doldrums. New trade routes to the riches of the East, around the Cape of Good Hope, and from the Americas and the Caribbean brought new cargoes, and consequently took all the best investment.

Without their old enemies,
the Ottoman Turks, to fight
against, the Order seemed to
lose its focus, becoming dis-
solute and tired. The French
Revolution of 1789, and the
subsequent downfall of the
aristocracy and the church in
France, shook the Order to
the core, for it deprived the
Knights of much of their
support – and a major part
of their revenue.

French forces land on Malta

Enter Napoleon

In 1798, Napoleon Bona-
parte avariciously eyed the Mediterranean and came to the
same conclusion reached by many commanders before and
since: Malta would be valuable to him, and it would pose a
serious threat if it were to fall into the hands of his enemies.
On 9 June his armada of 472 ships carrying 5,000 soldiers
gathered along the coastline and, on the pretext of entering
the harbour for provisions, Napoleon and some troops
landed. He presented the Knights with a simple order: they
must pack up and leave. Where others had failed, Napoleon
succeeded. Grand Master von Hompesch had no stomach
for a fight and simply did as he was ordered. After 268 years
in residence, the world's most famous military order departed without any action to defend its stronghold.

Two years of French rule followed, in which the arrogant
behaviour of the occupiers made them hated by both the
Maltese and the Church. A popular insurrection began, and
as the Maltese began to rebel, so a delegation was sent to
Naples to request help from the British Navy which was

based there while preparing to pursue and destroy the French fleet. Britain was at war with France and, appreciating the islanders' need for help in their uprising, both the King of Naples and Admiral Horatio Nelson sent troops and ships to Malta. The islands' harbours were blockaded by the massed ships and troops were landed. Against such odds the French commander surrendered and the French force left the islands, taking with them many treasures they had looted. On 5 September 1800 the British flag flew over Valletta.

Britain informally administered the islands for the remainder of the ongoing Napoleonic Wars and British possession of the islands was formally recognised in the Treaty of Paris in 1814, and again at the Congress of Vienna.

British Colony

In 1813 – a year marked by a plague that killed off one-fifth of Malta's inhabitants – Sir Thomas Maitland arrived as governor. Nicknamed 'King Tom', he dismissed the traditional self-governing Università and introduced sweeping reforms to bring the legal system into line with the English one. A period of stability followed which saw new crops introduced, more

British ship in Grand Harbour

vineyards planted, and water resources managed more efficiently, resulting in increased crop yields. The building of bases for the Royal Navy that patrolled the expanding British Empire boosted both employment and prosperity. The opening of the Suez Canal in 1869 increased shipping in the Mediterranean, and by 1880 Grand Harbour was a major port.

The Maltese, however, had not lost their desire to achieve independence, and during the 19th century a succession of constitutions gave the people varying degrees of autonomy. Riots following World War I brought about real change, codified in the new Constitution of 1921. The Maltese became responsible for their own internal affairs, while London retained control of defence, foreign affairs and matters affecting the Empire.

The Second Great Siege

Malta was vital to the Allied cause during World War II. Not only could ships and aircraft based here block the deployment of Italy's navy, they could also attack supply routes to the German and Italian forces operating from North Africa. When Italy under Benito Mussolini entered the war on 10 June 1940, his first move was to bomb Malta. During 1941, Italian, and later German, aircraft kept up almost incessant daily raids.

As General Rommel advanced through Egypt in the spring of 1942, air attacks increased, and in March and April the islands were hit with more than twice the weight of bombs that fell on London during any full year of the war. Life became increasingly miserable, with people living in cellars and caves in conditions of near-starvation.

This second great siege in Malta's history was only relieved in August 1942 with the arrival of a convoy of ships carrying fuel and supplies. Only five ships out of the original 13 made it from Britain, but it was enough to save the island and the Allied foothold in the area.

The George Cross

In recognition of the bravery and sacrifice shown by the Maltese in World War II, the island was awarded Britain's highest honour for civilian gallantry – the George Cross. It is shown on the national flag.

Independence

The price of freedom had been high: thousands of people killed or injured, and thousands of homes destroyed. After the war, Britain gave Malta financial help for reconstruction, and a new constitution granted the islands self-government within the Commonwealth. Plans for the complete transfer of power met with difficulties, but on 21 September 1964, Malta became fully independent for the first time in recorded history. Her parliament declared a republic in 1974.

In 1979, British forces bade farewell to Malta. Although the islanders welcomed independence, many had depended on the British services for their livelihood, and the island quickly needed to find other forms of revenue.

Tourism seemed to be a perfect choice. The climate, along with the wealth of historical buildings, would guarantee visitors, and Malta benefited from an explosion in European air travel in the 1970s and 1980s. This rush to develop a tourist infrastructure has not always resulted in the best-planned or prettiest modern resorts, but in the 1990s the Maltese began to make efforts to do justice to their older architectural beauty. Innovative tourism ventures and a cruise-ship terminal reinforce Malta's position as a prime tourist destination.

Pageant at Fort St Elmo

Malta joined the European Union in May 2004, taking its place alongside other, much larger countries with a mixture of popular enthusiasm and trepidation. And on 1 January 2008, the euro was introduced. Yet another chapter is being added to the islands' rich history.

Historical Landmarks

5300BC Settlers arrive, probably across a land bridge from Sicily.

4100BC onwards The first temples are built.

8th century BC The Phoenicians settle the islands.

550–218BC Malta is ruled by Carthage, a former Phoenician colony.

218BC The islands become part of the Roman Empire.

AD60 St Paul and St Luke are shipwrecked off Malta.

5th and 6th centuries Malta is conquered by Goths and Vandals.

870 The islands are conquered by the Aghlabid Caliphs. The Arabic language is adopted along with the Islamic religion.

1127 Malta reconquered by King Roger the Norman, and the islands become part of the Christian Kingdom of Sicily.

1266 The French House of Anjou takes over Sicily and Malta.

1282–1530 Aragonese rule Sicily and Malta.

1530 Emperor Charles V gives Malta to the Order of St John.

1546 and **1551** Privateers from the Barbary Coast attack Gozo.

1565 The Great Siege. Suleiman the Magnificent's Ottoman fleet lays siege to Malta for three months, but is unsuccessful.

1566 Construction work begins on the new capital, Valletta.

1798 Napoleon takes Malta without a fight. The Knights are forced out.

1800 The Maltese call the British fleet under Admiral Nelson to their aid. The islands' British period begins.

1814–64 As a British colony, Malta becomes an important naval base.

1869 The Suez Canal opens; Malta at the forefront of Mediterranean trade.

1919 The 'Bread Rebellion' breaks out on 7 June as a result of British pricing policies on imported grain. Several people die.

1921 Britain grants Malta its own constitution and partial self-government.

1934 Maltese becomes an official language alongside English.

1939–43 Malta is bombed severely during World War II. In recognition of Maltese heroism, Britain awards the islands the George Cross.

1964 Malta gains its independence in the Commonwealth.

1974 Proclamation of the Republic of Malta.

2004 Malta becomes a member of the European Union.

WHERE TO GO

The Maltese islands are compact and relatively easy to explore either independently, in a rental car, on public transport or by an organised tour. We will begin by looking at the largest island, Malta – including Valletta, the towns around Valletta and the Grand Harbour. Other sections of the book will explore the southeast coast before moving inland. Finally, we will journey along the northern coast before sailing across the water to Comino and Gozo, the other inhabited islands.

VALLETTA

When the Order of St John first settled on Malta in 1530 they made their home at Birgu (today's Vittoriosa) in the Grand Harbour where the Maltese community lived. It was sheltered and had deepwater creeks for merchant ships. Across the harbour, separating it from the equally large Marsamxett Harbour with its fishing community, lay the barren Sceberras peninsula with a small fortress, Fort St Elmo, at its tip. As the fort guarded the entrance to the harbours, they set about reinforcing its battlements to make it impregnable.

In 1565, however, when the Ottoman force landed, it set up its mortars on the peninsula's high ground and rained fire on to St Elmo below. The Knights and their Maltese compatriots put up some courageous resistance, but ultimately all but four of the defenders were killed. The Turks then turned all their fire on to the fortified community that lay across the harbour – Birgu, Bormla (today's Cospicua) and l'Isla (Senglea). The Knights were finally victorious and the siege was lifted, but lessons had been learned. Plans were speedily made to create

One of the views from the Upper Barrakka Gardens

a new fortified city on the dominating heights of the peninsula. The city would be called **Valletta** in honour of Grand Master La Valette who led the islands to victory.

A simple yet effective design was created. The city would have towering bastion walls encircling it, with two defensive emplacements known as Cavaliers where troops would be stationed overlooking a dry moat near the landside entrance to the city. The newly restored, much larger Fort St Elmo would guard the sea approach. Within the city walls all streets would run in a grid pattern with palaces, churches and the *auberges* where each group of knights or *langue* would live, given due prominence. It would be a gracious city, built with the generous monies sent by the grateful monarchs of Europe who had seen the spread of the Ottoman Empire so successfully halted.

Work began in 1566 from plans drawn up by Francesco Laparelli, architect to the Vatican and the Medici family. He promised that the city could be constructed in a mere three months, but when he returned to Italy two years later there was still a great deal to be done. The project was left in the hands of his Maltese assistant, Gerolamo Cassar, who finished the work, and also added his own imprint on the city.

Balcony views

During the 18th century, in order to give privacy to wives and daughters watching daily life in the streets, many city buildings were furnished with *gallarija*, wooden balconies. Lines of these balconies – which undulate with the rise and fall of streets – are one of the city's enduring images.

Following the departure of the Knights of St John at the end of the 18th century, many of Valletta's beautiful buildings were taken for other civil or military uses. Today, though Valletta has moved on into modern times, the initial *raison d'être* for the creation of the city can still clearly be seen. The walls and bastions still stand strong; and to see the city

Fort St Angelo *(left)* faces Valletta across Grand Harbour

from the air, or from the waters of the Grand Harbour or Marsamxett Harbour, really brings home the amazing feat of the builders. In 1980, the city of Valletta was designated a UNESCO World Heritage Site.

City Gate

Valletta is less than one kilometre (⅔ mile) wide and 1.5km (1 mile) long. The main entrance, the **City Gate**, cuts the old walls, but it has little architectural value as its original Baroque gate was demolished in the 1960s to make access easier. It has now been pedestrianised, however, and because it leads to the main bus terminal it is always busy with people and stalls selling cool drinks and snacks. The gate sits at the top of the main road through the city, **Triq il-Republikka** (Republic Street), and exploring its attractions makes a good start for your tour. The upper section is relatively flat, then drops down towards Fort St Elmo jutting out to sea.

Republic Street is a pleasant thoroughfare with several fine buildings as well as shops and cafés. There is a tourist information office immediately through City Gate on your right.

Strolling down the street, which was known as Strada Reale during the Knights' days and Kingsway under British rule, you will first notice the ruins of what would have been a large building; vestiges of classical columns can still be seen. This was the site of the **Royal Opera House**, which was bombed in 1942 and never rebuilt.

Further along on your left, you will find the Auberge de Provence, finished in 1575 and now housing the **National Museum of Archaeology** (open daily 9am–5pm; closed public holidays; admission fee). The building itself is interesting, being one of the *auberges* that the public can still enter, but the collections it displays are also fascinating and add extra detail to the bare bones of dates and eras of the islands' prehistory. The Neolithic and Bronze Ages are brought to life.

Ancient Malta

A timeline close to the doorway of the National Museum of Archaeology points out that the Maltese temple sites were built over 1,000 years before the pyramids in Egypt.

Beautiful pottery effigies and stone carvings found at Tarxien and other archaeological sites bear witness to the sophistication of these ancient peoples. Upstairs the collection focuses on more recent history, featuring finds from the Roman era.

St John's Co-Cathedral

Then you come to one of the most important buildings in Valletta, the **Co-Cathedral of St John** (open Mon–Fri 9.30am–4pm, Sat–Sun 9.30am–1pm; admission fee) dedicated by the Knights to their Maltese architect Gerolamo Cassar. Turn right here on St John's Street to find its main entrance. Cassar designed the church, which was constructed between 1573 and 1577, and his plan surrounded the building with a number of small open squares.

The severe façade of the church belies the ornate beauty within – it is a magnificent decorative masterpiece. Small chapels off the main nave are dedicated to each *langue*, and the floor of the church consists of tombs of knights, highly decorated with coloured marble. The vault is decorated with several huge frescoes by Mattia Preti (1613–90), an Italian artist favoured by the Order during his lifetime, featuring scenes from the life of St John the Baptist.

The church, which was granted cathedral status by Pope Pius VII in 1816 (the name Co-Cathedral indicates it belonged to a convent or religious order), also has a museum with beautiful Flemish tapestries and other works of art, including Malta's greatest treasure, *The Beheading of St John the Baptist* by Caravaggio. It is a masterpiece of great drama.

St John's Co-Cathedral

Republic Square

Beyond the Cathedral on Republic Street you will find a small square now called **Republic Square**, which has at its centre a rather solemn statue of Queen Victoria, usually sporting a pigeon on top of her tiny crown. In fine weather, she is surrounded by a sea of parasols, and tables put out by nearby cafés where you can enjoy lunch or a drink and watch the world go by.

The buildings on the square are beautifully colonnaded but the eye is drawn to a very ornate façade that is its backdrop. This fine Baroque building, the last to be constructed by the Knights, was finished in 1796. It was originally intended to house the large collection of books owned by the Order, designated as a Bibliotheca Publica (Public Library) in 1760, and is now called the **National Library**. For those with a particular interest in the Knights of St John, the library is a treasure trove of information and artefacts. In addition to a large collection of books, including more than 45 printed before 1500, there are charters and documents relating to the workings of the Order, including the original Deed of Donation of Malta to the Order in 1530.

Among the colonnades running below the library is

The Queen Victoria monument at Republic Square

Café Premier, a popular place for coffee and romantic trysts. In the late 1990s the café was totally refurbished and is now a smart patisserie. Next door is **The Great Siege of Malta and The Knights of St John Experience** (open daily 10am–4pm; admission fee). This walk-through exhibition charts the history of the Order from their earliest days in Jerusalem, to staging points in Cyprus and Rhodes before their arrival in Malta. It then brings to life the fight with the Ottoman Turks and the building of Valletta. Life-size figures depict the major characters involved and you travel through Suleiman's court, on an Ottoman ship bringing soldiers to fight the Knights, and then enter the battlefield itself. The displays are enhanced by a well-produced soundtrack and film re-enactments. The attraction has the patronage of the present Grand Master of the Sovereign Military Order of Malta.

Palace of the Grand Masters

Next to the Republic Square is the huge façade of the **Palace of the Grand Masters**, once the official and private residence of the Grand Master of the Order of St John. The palace, with its 100-metre-long façade, was constructed between 1572 and 1580 with one entrance arch (near Archbishop Street). Later in the 18th century Grand Master Pinto added the second entrance and the long balconies that grace each corner. Today the palace is the president's office and seat of the Maltese Parliament.

A visit to the **State Rooms** (open daily 10am–5pm, subject to state functions; admission fee; tel: 2124 9349), in the same way as a visit to St John's Co-Cathedral, brings to life the wealth and power of the Order of St John. Overlooking Neptune's Courtyard, the fine rooms of the *piano nobile* (first floor) are linked by corridors decorated with frescoes, armour and portraits. An impressive door leads into the **Throne Room**, sometimes called the Hall of St Michael and St George,

Inside the Armoury at the Grand Master's Palace

which was the Order's Supreme Council Chamber. Its frieze, painted after 1576, depicts 12 incidents in the Great Siege. To one side is the **Red Room**, which was the Grand Master's audience chamber, and to the other side is the **Yellow Room** where pages would wait to be summoned. Also here is the **State Dining Room** and the **Tapestry Chamber**, which was the Order's Council Chamber. The Gobelin tapestries on the walls were presented in 1697.

On the ground floor is the **Armoury** (open daily 9am–5pm; closed public holidays; admission fee). The collection of 6,000 pieces includes remarkable suits of armour made for Grand Masters, arms used in the Great Siege of 1565, and a rare hide and copper cannon, along with pikes and shields. Grand Master Wignacourt's ceremonial suit is inlaid with gold.

North of the palace, Republic Street drops down towards Fort St Elmo. A series of wide, shallow marble steps flank the roadway here. Be careful, because they can be slippery in wet weather. At No. 74 Republic Street you will find **Casa Rocca Piccola** (admission fee), a house built in the 16th century and now the home of a noble family. The interior is typical of house design at the time, including an interior courtyard with stairs leading to a *piano nobile* or first-floor living area. The rooms are full of antiques, including a portable altar that folds neatly into a chest of drawers for travelling.

Fort St Elmo

Where the road ends you reach **Fort St Elmo** (open Sun 11am
for 'In Guardia' re-enactment; admission fee). This huge fortification – pride of the Knights of St John – was rebuilt and
extended after being overrun in the siege of 1565 and was further fortified in 1687. The round stone slabs at the entrance
to the fort are the covers of huge underground grain stores,
each of which could hold 5,000 tons of food. Flat stones shield
the openings against rain and prevent modern visitors from
falling into the stores. The fort, which was upgraded several
times during British rule, last saw action in World War II and
shows evidence of almost every era of its existence.

Vendome Bastion, a part of the fort once used to store gun-
powder, is now the **National War Museum** (open daily 9am–
5pm; closed public holidays; admission fee). Enter through
an arch some 50m (55yds) west of the fort's main entrance.
The museum, dedicated in 1975, tells the story of Malta's second great siege in World War II, and her role in the Allies'
eventual success in 1945. Photographs show the devastation
caused by Axis bombing and relate the stories of heroism by
Maltese nationals and servicemen. Hundreds of relics are on
view, from the Gloster Gladiator biplane 'Faith' – one of only

'In Guardia'

Every Sunday between September and June, Fort St Elmo comes alive
with the sound of clashing swords and musket fire in a historical parade
and re-enactment called 'In Guardia'.

It offers visitors an opportunity to step back in time to the era of the
heroic Knights of Malta – to an age when the fortress was new and perhaps the most impregnable in the world. The event is a breathtaking
spectacle of colour and noise, starting at 11am. For exact dates contact
the Malta Tourist Authority, tel: 2123 7747.

three on hand to protect the island at the start of hostilities – to ration books and gas masks. Pride of place goes to the **George Cross**, awarded to Malta in 1942 in recognition of the islanders' bravery in the face of continued attacks.

Marsamxett Side of Republic Street

Now that we have explored the attractions along Republic Street, we can head out to the other parts of the city. The attractions are not difficult to find on the narrow streets, and we'll look first at those on the streets to the left of Republic Street (the northern Marsamxett side), then to the right (southern, Grand Harbour side).

On South Street at the City Gate end of Republic Street is the **National Museum of Fine Arts** (open daily 9am–5pm; closed public holidays; admission fee), housed in the residence of Fra Jean de Soubiran, which was completed in 1571 and later acquired by the Order. During British rule it was the residence of the Naval Commander-in-Chief, a very important military position. The building is interesting in itself, with a stairway decorated in an ornamental Baroque style. The museum has 24 rooms displaying a wide range of European art. Two rooms are given over to the works of Mattia Preti. A curious collection of Knights' memorabilia can be found in the basement. These include coins, religious relics and model ships.

As the threat of the Turks subsided, the Knights began to look for worldly pleasures to fill their time and in 1731, the then Grand Master, Manoel de Vilhena, commissioned a theatre for the city. The **Manoel Theatre** (open daily 9am–5pm; billed as Teatru Manoel) opened a year later and presented plays and operas until the Royal Opera House opened in 1861. The Royal Opera House was demolished during World War II and never rebuilt, but the Manoel, in Old Theatre Street, having fallen into disrepair, was completely refurbished at government expense in 1960. Today its beautifully decorated stalls and elliptical ceiling are well worth seeing, as are many productions. There are regular guided tours so you don't need to wait for a performance. Alongside the theatre, and dominating the Valletta skyline, is the **Church of Our Lady of Mount Carmel**, which was completed in 1958 on the site of a Cassar-designed church that was also badly damaged during World War II. The dome is 73m (240ft) high and dominates the spire of **St Paul's Anglican Cathedral**, built on the site of the Auberge d'Allemagne with funds donated by Queen Adelaide, consort of William IV, in 1839.

Grand Harbour Side of Republic Street

A number of interesting buildings are situated to the Grand Harbour side of Republic Street. If you enter the city by car you will find yourself facing one of the most beautiful

St Paul's spire and Our Lady of Mount Carmel's dome

Upper Barrakka Gardens

historic buildings of Valletta, the **Auberge de Castille**. Constructed in 1574, it was home to knights from Castile, Leon and Portugal. Grand Master Emanuel Pinto De Fonseca added the beautifully ornamented façade in 1744 in the fashionable Baroque style of the time. The *auberge* now serves as the office of the Maltese prime minister, and although it is a superb example of Baroque architecture, there is no public access.

From the *auberge*, head right, past the small Greek revival style building – the Malta Stock Exchange – to **Upper Barrakka Gardens**, ◀ once a private garden of the Knights but today offering local people and visitors alike the most spectacular views of the Grand Harbour. The Gardens sit on the St Peter and St Paul Bastion and were laid out in the 17th century. Numerous plaques and sculptures adorn the flower beds but most people head out to the open terrace, camera in hand. The view is a spectacular panorama stretching from Fort Ricasoli facing Fort St Elmo at the harbour's entrance on your left to deep into the harbour's reaches on your right, where Malta's dockyard repairs international shipping. Facing you is historic Fort St Angelo and the Three Cities.

Follow St Paul Street alongside Castille until you reach the **Church of St Paul Shipwrecked**. Designed by Gerolamo

Cassar, this is one of the oldest churches in Valletta, and has several paintings by Attilio Palombi depicting scenes from the saint's life. A large wooden statue adorns the interior and the church safeguards a jewelled reliquary that contains a relic of the saint's wrist and a piece of the column on which St Paul is believed to have been martyred.

Back on the city wall at the Grand Harbour side (from St Paul's Street walk down several flights of stairs) is **Lower Barrakka Gardens**. This also offers a view across the harbour, but gives a different perspective with a vista of Fort Ricasoli at the mouth of Grand Harbour. In the centre of the gardens is monument like a Doric temple, erected as a memorial to Sir Alexander Ball, who led the blockade that defeated the French in 1800.

Below you is the Siege Bell memorial, unveiled by Queen Elizabeth II during a visit to Malta in 1992. It is dedicated to the men who lost their lives in the 1940–3 wartime convoys. From the bell you can clearly see the long plain façade of the **Sacra Infermeria**, once the hospital run by the Knights – one of the most advanced medical facilities of its day when it opened in 1574. The hospital was used as a medical facility until after World War I. The huge wards – the longest measured 161m (528ft) – are now home to the **Mediterranean Conference Centre** (open daily; admission fee), one of Malta's success stories since independence, which hosts several major international conferences a year.

Malta Experience

Next to the Mediterranean Conference Centre is The Malta Experience (hourly programmes Mon–Fri 11am–4pm, Sat–Sun 11am–1pm; admission fee), a multi-media spectacular which takes viewers on a 50-minute journey through the history of the islands. It is a great way to get your bearings and an excellent introduction to the sights and sites of Malta.

OUTSIDE VALLETTA

Valletta does not have a monopoly on history or wonderful architecture. Almost every town or village on the islands will have a building – often a church – that is worthy of note and exploration. The countryside is also littered with military remains. These include forts and towers from the time of the Knights as well as 19th- and 20th-century fortifications.

Floriana

Any trip to Valletta will entail travelling through Floriana, situated just outside the gates of the capital. Floriana is named after military engineer Pietro Floriani, who was charged with the job of extending Valletta's defences in the mid-16th century, so giving rise to the creation of this suburb. Floriana was rebuilt after World War II, and her finest buildings were faithfully recreated.

The gateway marking the entrance to Floriana sits astride two lanes of a main road that bisects the town. Called the **Portes des Bombes**, it was built in 1721 as part of Valletta's outer ring of defence, but has undergone several alterations since then. In the 19th century roads were cut through the bastion walls on either side to speed the flow of traffic.

The dome that dominates the skyline belongs to **St Publius Church**, named after the 'headman' of Malta at the time when the apostle Paul was shipwrecked on the island while on a voyage to Rome (as a prisoner of the Romans) in AD60. Publius invited St Paul to stay in his home, and St Paul is said to have repaid the kindness by healing his father of an illness. He also made Publius one of his first converts to Christianity, and Publius went on to become the first Bishop of Malta. The square in front of the church has granary silos under its surface, dating from 1660, that were in continual use until the 1960s.

The Portes des Bombes leads into Floriana

Rinella

Facing Fort St Elmo across the Grand Harbour is **Fort Rica-soli**, with its beautiful gate dated 1698. Now in disrepair, it is used by film companies to build large-scale open-air sets. Both *Gladiator* and *Troy* were filmed here; for *Gladiator* the replica of the Colosseum was built in the large central space.

Further east around the point is **Fort Rinella** (open daily 9am–5pm; military re-enactments include firing of howitzers; admission fee). This 19th-century fort was built to house the largest cannon ever built – a 100-ton gun that no other forti-fication could accommodate. The muzzle-loader required a team of 22 people to man it in action, and it could penetrate 38cm (15in) of metal at a distance of 8km (5 miles). Next to the fort is the **Mediterranean Film Studios** (tours available) which opened in 1963. Several major films as well as TV dra-mas, commercials and music videos have been made at the stu-dios, which have the largest water tank facilities in Europe.

The Vittoriosa waterfront

The Three Cities

When the Order of St John took up residence in the Grand Harbour, they settled in Birgu and its suburb, Bormla. A small community lived on the neighbouring promontory, l'Isla. After the Great Siege victory, Birgu became known as Vittoriosa (the victorious one), Bormla became Cospicua (Conspicuous) and l'Isla, the island, became Senglea, named after Grand Master Claude de la Sengle, who divided the land for it to be used for Maltese dwellings. Although the traffic signs say Vittoriosa, Cospicua and Senglea, many Maltese use the original names: Birgu, Bormla and l'Isla. They were designated Cities during the brief French occupation.

The first military action the Knights carried out on arrival was the reinforcement of the old fortification jutting out into the harbour. This they renamed **Fort St Angelo**.

In 1565 this fort withstood repeated Turkish attacks, its defenders consisting of 600 knights and fewer than 1,000 men-at-arms. Reinforced after the victory, the fort has remained unchanged in outline since 1689. It was used as a naval station by the British (who renamed it HMS St Angelo). The Maltese government has leased part of the fort back to the Sovereign Military Order of Malta, so much of the upper bastions are now off limits to visitors.

The town of **Vittoriosa** sits behind the fort. Vittoriosa Square is diminutive but forms a central point for several thoroughfares through the town – the streets are still laid out as they were in medieval times, with bends and curves rather than straight lines. Birgu developed according to the needs of the Knights. Seven *auberges* and a hospital were built here, though these facilities were later transferred to Valletta. A convent built beside the hospital still has a community of sisters, more than 400 years later, and a bishop's palace built in 1542, which now serves as a school.

Then, in 1574, another more powerful servant of the church arrived to oversee the deeds of the Knights and the Maltese population: the Inquisitor. He took up offices in what had previously been the Law Courts and embellished the building. The Inquisition was all-powerful until it was abolished by the French in 1798. Grand Inquisitors were charged with the responsibility of investigating any evidence of heresy. This they did with ruthless efficiency. They also acted as arbitrators in the case of disputes between the Knights, Grand Master, and the Bishop. The plain façade of the **Inquisitor's Palace** (open daily 9am–5pm; closed

Inside the Inquisitor's Palace

public holidays; admission fee) houses plain prison cells and dungeons on the lower floors, which contrast with the highly decorated private apartments of the Inquisitors themselves above, including the Tribunal room where evidence was heard and verdicts were issued.

On the waterfront, with its impressive Cottonera Marina full of sleek yachts and cruisers, stands the **church of St Lawrence**. The original edifice, which dates from 1530, has been adapted and embellished over the centuries, including the addition of a Baroque façade. Inside, an altarpiece by Mattia Preti graces one of nine altars. Outside the church is the **Freedom Monument**, with bronze figures depicting the departure of the last British serviceman who stepped on to a naval vessel from this wharf in 1979.

Along Vittoriosa waterfront

Enter the wharf under the arch at the waterside here. This area was a hive of activity under British rule, as Malta was a major naval and military outpost of the Empire. The British built a large victualling yard and bakery along the wharf to restock the ships and feed the garrison. Following their closure in 1979, the buildings were allowed to fall into decay but part of the naval bakery has been refurbished to house the **National Maritime Museum** (open daily 9am–5pm; closed pub-

lic holidays; admission fee).
Here you will find displays
of artifacts salvaged in Maltese waters, along with naval
uniforms and paintings. The
naval tactic textbooks and
models of ships on display
were used in the training
of naval cadets. There is
also a section on traditional
Maltese craft.

Vittoriosa was protected
on the landward side by a
wall consisting of a series of
bastions and curtains (sheer
walls). Three gateways al-

The vedette at Senglea

lowed entry and can still be seen. The only remaining gate in
use is the pedestrianised **Couvre Port** dating from 1727.

Facing Vittoriosa, and also jutting into the harbour, is **Senglea**, named after Grand Master Claude de la Sengle who
built its fortifications in 1551. **Safe Haven Garden**, at the
very tip, offers good views across the harbour to the Valletta
skyline. It is protected by a recreated stone **vedette** atop a
bastion, decorated by an eye and an ear indicating that it is
all-seeing and all-hearing.

Today Senglea is a working city. Most of its population
travels to the Malta Dockyard at Frenchmen's Creek. The
tradition of shipbuilding and repair carries on into modern
times, with huge cranes and jacks on the move every day.

Cospicua, between Senglea and Vittoriosa, was the largest
of the three cities in the 16th century but was badly damaged
in World War II, and was rebuilt as an industrial town.

All three cities were bound together in a huge fortification
built in the 1680s when the Grand Master Nicola Cottoner

commissioned and paid for a massive outer protective wall in case of another attack. About 3km (2 miles) of wall stretched from the waters of Kalkara Creek (north of Vittoriosa) to Frenchmen's Creek. There were five entry gates; the central one has a bust of Cottoner and beautiful embellishments in stone. The new walls, which came to be known as the **Cottonera Lines**, can clearly be seen as you travel the area, and are as impressive now as they would have been to a Turkish janissary in the 17th century.

The Hypogeum and the Tarxien Temples

Paola and Tarxien are two busy towns, 10 minutes by car from Valletta. Within their boundaries they have two very important ancient sites, both discovered in the early 19th century. The **Ħal-Saflieni Hypogeum** (conducted tours only, daily every hour between 8.30am and 3.30pm, 2.30pm on Sun) began life as a simple cave where Neolithic settlers buried their dead (hypogeum is a Greek word meaning underground). Sometime between 3800 and 2500BC, the population began to cut and shape the cave, creating a second level of chambers, and later a third, until the caves reached downwards 12m (40ft) underground. The sheer scale of the hypogeum is astounding, and the workmanship involved is evidence of the sophistication of these ancient peoples. The remains of more than 7,000 people have been found here, and many artefacts excavated are now on display at the National Museum of Archae-

Hypogeum tours

The Hypogeum's microclimate is strictly regulated to ensure its conservation. For this reason, the site is open to no more than 80 visitors a day. Booking for the tours well in advance is advised (tel: 2180 5019; info@ heritagemalta.org; tickets are also available from the Hypogeum visitor centre in Paola and National Museum of Archaeology in Valletta).

ology in Valletta. The tour of the site starts with a brief introductory exhibition and a multilingual audio-visual film focusing on the temple-building peoples and the Hypogeum's relationship to Malta's temple sites.

The nearby **Tarxien Temples** (pronounced Tar-sheen; open daily 9am–5pm; closed public holidays; admission fee) provide a very important archaeological record of Maltese life in the 4th millennium BC. They were discovered in 1915, when a farmer, concerned about the huge stones that littered his fields, called someone to investigate the situation. Dr Themistocles Zammit, a Maltese archaeologist arrived and excavated the whole site to discover three temples. There is no record of the farmer's reaction.

Pre-historic spiral stone decoration at Tarxien

The Tarxien Temples show evidence of the great strides forward made during the temple building phases by builders whose only tools were axes and flints; trees were used to lever the stones into position. The middle temple, which dates from 3200BC, is more substantial and accurate than earlier ones at Ġgantija on Gozo. Libation holes, used to worship the gods of the underworld, can clearly be seen, but the many carved stone slabs depicting bulls and pigs are copies – the originals can be seen at the National Museum of Archaeology in Valletta.

The town of Tarxien is also interesting, for although the modern suburbs crowd the temple site, the heart of the old town is charming, its buildings little changed over centuries.

Sliema, St Julians and Paceville

These are the holiday destinations for many visitors to the islands. **Sliema** on the shore of Marsamxett Harbour facing Valletta was, until the 1970s, the island's only resort area. But as tourism developed, so St Julians and Paceville further along the coastline began to take over with an ever-increasing wide variety of hotels, restaurants, cafés and bars. This is the area that comes to life at night and buzzes until the early hours.

Sliema started out as a sheltered fishing village, but as people began to find Valletta too hot in the summer months, so they built themselves houses in Sliema in order to enjoy the cooler air by the sea. The village grew into a modern, sophisticated town, and now apartments in its tall buildings that line the promenade facing the sea command seriously high prices. There are fine hotels and shops, and from its harbour cruise boats set out daily for tours around the islands and harbours. There is even a disco boat or two that sails by night.

As more land was required for houses, Sliema expanded to become linked with **St Julians**, a fishing village further north along the coast. Its picturesque bay is now edged with restaurants and St Julians has become the place to be.

Joining St Julians is **Paceville**, the nightlife centre that never seems to sleep. There are bars, discos, cinemas and a wide variety of restaurants, from inexpensive to costly. If you are young, Paceville is where you come.

On the perimeter is tranquil **St George's Bay**, with luxurious, modern five-star hotels and beach lidos. Jutting out to sea is the **Dragonara Casino**, with gaming tables in the elegant setting of a summer palazzo once owned by a marquis.

THE SOUTHEAST

The southeastern section of Malta is an interesting mixture of old and new, where tradition carries on alongside 21st-century industry. A number of bays offer shelter for boats, especially Marsaxlokk and Marsascala. This is where you will find the fishing fleets – and some of the best fish restaurants. **Marsascala** is the most easterly town on Malta. Its little fishing boats bob on the water of its picturesque narrow bay. With its simple restaurants and cafés it has developed into a tranquil resort.

Marsaxlokk

To the south of Marsaskala is **Marsaxlokk** (mar-sash-lok), with the largest fishing fleet in Malta. Marsaxlokk Bay is the islands' largest bay, and traditional, brightly-painted Maltese fishing boats such as the *luzzu* sit on the water or rest on the dockside. You'll find the fisherman tending to the boats or mending nets, constantly chatting as they work. Fish restaurants have tables by the water where you can enjoy an alfresco lunch or dinner, and there is a daily market here with table linens and lace for sale.

If you head out towards the lighthouse and fort at Delimara Point, you will

The picturesque harbour at Marsaxlokk

The Eye of Osiris

All traditional brightly-coloured fishing boats in Maltese waters have an eye painted at each side of their bow. This is to ward off any evil that may be out at sea. Osiris was god of fertility and of the dead. Here he wards off evil in the company of saints as most boats are named after saints and carry little shrines. Every spring, before the fishermen put their boats on the water for the summer, they will paint the eye afresh to give them maximum protection.

pass the Carmelite church of **Tas-Silġ**, a site of religious worship for many centuries before the birth of Christ. Unfortunately, this area has been spoiled visually by a new power station.

Għar Dalam

On the edge of Birżebbuġa is the fascinating cave system of **Għar Dalam** with a small museum that displays finds from the site (open daily 9am–5pm; closed public holidays; admission fee). Għar Dalam cave runs for 144m (472ft) into the limestone rock and its fissures link to caves in the west that once formed part of an ancient water course.

During the Pleistocene period this area was a haven for hippopotami, dwarf elephants, micro-mammals and birds, whose remains were fossilised over hundreds of thousands of years. The bones indicate that Malta was once rich in water and vegetation and joined to what is now the European mainland. Above the pebble layer is the so-called 'deer' layer, dated to approximately 18,000 years ago. The top layer, or 'cultural layer', dates to less than 10,000 years ago and holds evidence of the first humans on the island. The museum displays thousands of specimens in glass cases.

Birżebbuġa (bir-zeb-boo-ja) has some tourist infrastructure; however, its best beach at Pretty Bay has been blighted by the building of a modern container freeport nearby. Malta is the perfect central depot for container traffic in the Mediterranean and the Malta Freeport tranships goods and oil from all corners of the world.

Malta International Airport cuts a swathe across this southeastern area. **Żurrieq** is the largest of the small villages that lie on the far side of the airfield. It has a pretty church dedicated to St Catherine (1659). Inside is a charming altarpiece by Mattia Preti, who also decorated St John's Co-Cathedral in Valletta.

Blue Grotto

Follow the coast road and you come to picturesque **Wied-iż-Żurrieq**, a fjord-like inlet in the dramatic coastline where there is a tiny fishing village used by a handful of fisherman whose colourful boats you will see bobbing in the water or pulled up on the steep hillside for repair. A number of small craft leave the narrow concrete slip that acts as a jetty for tours to the **Blue Grotto** (open daily in daylight hours, weather permitting; boat hire fee for the

Excursion to the Blue Grotto

30-minute trip) and the rugged coastline. The best time to see the grotto is early in the day before the sun gets too high. Because of its unusual charm Wied-iż-Żurrieq is a popular destination for tour groups who flock into the simple cafés for refreshments and souvenirs.

Ħaġar Qim and Mnajdra

A short distance away on the road leading along the cliffs are the spectacular Neolithic remains of **Ħaġar Qim** and **Mnajdra** (both open daily 9am–5pm; closed public holidays; admission fee), on a hillside overlooking the tiny island of **Filfla**. The island is a bird sanctuary and is home to a unique species of lizard. Ħaġar Qim, which sits atop the cliffs, was discovered as early as 1839 and consists of a series of temples. Unfortunately it was constructed of soft stone and has weathered considerably. A number of 'fat lady' statuettes were found here indicating its use as a fertility shrine, and there are even tethering loops for animals in the stone but no one is sure if these were used for sacrifice. The 'fat ladies' are on display in the Archaeological Museum in Valletta.

Mnajdra (im-naydra) sits below Ħaġar Qim, around 500m (550yds) down a steep path.

Doorway detail, Ħaġar Qim

It is made up of two main temples dating from around 3400BC and is probably the best-preserved site on Malta. Its doorways are particularly fine, with posts and lintels. It is worthwhile climbing the slope behind the temples. From here you can get an overview of the whole site and appreciate its size and complicated structure.

Aerial view of Mdina outside Rabat

HEADING INLAND

If you are travelling from Valletta towards Mdina, you will
see the remains of the **Wignacourt Aqueduct**, which began
to supply water to Valletta in 1610.

Turn into Balzan to find **San Anton Palace and Gardens**,
built during the late 1620s as a summer palace for Grand
Master Antoine de Paule, who personally supervised the lay-
out of the formal gardens that surround it. Subsequent Grand
Masters added to the palace itself and the British contributed
the veranda beneath the turret. Filled with paintings and fine
art, the palace is now the official residence of the President
of Malta and, therefore, not open to visitors. The beautifully
kept San Anton Gardens are open to the public (free) and
contain palms, cypress, jacarandas, araucarias and other
exotic plants, some more than three centuries old, together
with graceful fountains, pools, statues and colourful flower-

beds. In addition there are glasshouses with indoor plants and an aviary. Various flower and animal shows are held here throughout the year, and there are open-air productions of Shakespeare by a local theatre group in the summer.

The main road continues to Mdina – you can see its walls and spires dominating the horizon. After a couple of minutes you will see a turning to the right, leading to **Ta' Qali Craft Village**, near the National Sports Stadium. Ta' Qali has a number of artisans working in what was formerly an air base. You'll see lace making, glass-blowing and potting, and will be able to buy straight from the manufacturer. It is being turned gradually into an attractive craft village.

Mdina's main gate and bridge

Mdina

Finally, the walls of **Mdina** loom large ahead. The Phoenicians called the town Maleth, and it was known in Roman times as Melita. In the 8th century, the Arabs transformed Mdina into a fortified citadel, building impregnable walls to protect it from enemy raids. Mdina (literally 'the walled city') was the capital of the island until the Knights of St John arrived in 1530 and made their headquarters at Grand Harbour; from then on it was simply referred to as Città Vecchia, the 'old city'.

During the Great Siege of 1565 the Turks concentrated

their efforts on Grand Harbour, giving the cavalry garrison at Mdina numerous opportunities for sorties that gradually wore down the enemy. Mdina also deterred the enemy by reinforcing the battlements with women disguised as soldiers – a ruse which completely deceived

Città Nobile

King Alphonse of Aragon conferred the title of Città Nobile on Mdina in 1428 after the city heroically withstood an attack by Islamic corsairs. In the raid 3,000 of the island's people were taken prisoner.

the Turks. Although Mdina lost its prestige as the island's capital under the Knights, it later became the see of the bishops, and was also allowed to remain the seat of the Università, the government advisory body made up of patricians and the clergy.

The city was badly damaged in an earthquake in 1693 and it was not until the 1720s that work began to rebuild and include some open spaces for the population to enjoy. While the street plan remains essentially medieval, with several fine period palaces, many of the public buildings date from the period of post-disaster Baroque building.

Magisterial Palace

When you step through the main gate of Mdina you step back in time. No neon signs or fast-food joints, no visitors' traffic. You can spend time wandering along the narrow alleys and the city walls – it takes only a few minutes to stroll the 400-m (1300-ft) length of the main street.

Just inside the main gate you will see the Magisterial Palace on your right. Built by Grand Master Manoel de Vilhena in the 1720s in French Baroque style, it was used as the seat of the commune – the local administrative assembly. The palace now houses the **National Museum of Natural History** (open daily 9am–5pm; closed public holidays; admission fee), with

Casa Inguanez door knocker

its collections of fossils, flora and fauna, and diagrams that explain the geology of the Maltese islands. Attached to the palace are buildings which once housed the law courts, and underneath these are the dungeons.

At the **Mdina Dungeons** exhibit you will see multifarious gory methods used to extract confessions, including the favoured forms of torture. As you go through the exhibit, don't forget that these are the actual buildings in which all this took place: the small cells would really have held human prisoners. The scenes of disfigurement and amputation are rather realistic, especially in conjunction with the spine-chilling sound effects, and so it may not be suitable for young children.

Villegaignon Street

Many of the main attractions can be found on **Villegaignon Street**, which cuts through the heart of the town. As you turn into Villegaignon Street, on your left is **Casa Inguanez**, the palace of the oldest noble family on Malta. Across the narrow street the **Chapel of St Agatha** is dedicated to the Christian martyr who came to Malta to escape Roman persecution in the 3rd century. The church dates from 1471 and was redesigned in 1694.

You will find several costumed ladies offering fliers for attractions as you walk down the street. Even in an area as small as Mdina there are several audio-visual walk-through attractions vying for your attention. Off Villegaignon Street, in historic Palazzo Gatto Murina, is **Tales of the Silent City**, which covers all aspects of Mdina's past. It also has a large gift shop and café. Down the narrow alleyway of Mesquita Street you can find **The Mdina Experience**, and on the old ramparts on Magazine Street is **The Knights of Malta**, which concentrates on the Order, its history and its role on the island.

Cathedral

The main square in the citadel is flanked on the western side by the **Cathedral of St Paul** (open Mon–Sat 9am–1pm, 2–4.30pm; free), said to have been built on the site where St Paul converted Publius, then the headman of the community, to Christianity in AD60. A church has existed on the site since the 4th century. This was enlarged under Count Roger's rule

The cathedral viewed from outside the walls

in 1090 and it was extended again in 1490. Following the earthquake of 1693 it was completely redesigned, although some features, such as the back arch of the church, and an Irish bogwood door dating from AD900, remain. The work was undertaken by Maltese architect Lorenzo Gafà and is a masterpiece, with columns, twin bell towers and a fine dome. Inside you will find a marble font dating from 1495, and a beautiful pavement of marble tombstones commemorating religious dignitaries. The painting by Mattia Preti depicting St Paul riding on a white charger recalls the time during the Saracen attack of 1494 when it is said that St Paul, mounted on a horse, appeared on the battlements of Mdina to frighten away the invaders.

Along Villegaignon Street to the Carmelite church

Across the small square outside the south door of the cathedral is the old **Seminary**. The main entrance of this majestic Baroque building, which dates from 1729, is flanked by two stone giants supporting an ornate stone balcony. Since 1968, the buildings have been used to house the **Cathedral Museum**, which has a wide ranging collection of religious artefacts and painting, including several medieval manuscripts and papal bulls relating to Malta. The museum also has an impressive numismatic collection that includes Maltese coins ranging from Carthaginian times to the present day.

From the cathedral, carry on along Villegaignon Street. You will be walking towards the corner statue of the Madonna and Child on the left, which adorns the **Carmelite Church**. Anti-French riots began here in 1798 when the French Commandant Masson indicated that he was going to plunder the treasury of the church.

The Greek Gate

Palazzo Falson

Opposite the church, a little further along the street, is **Palazzo Falson**, also known as 'Norman House' because of the shape of its windows. Now a museum (open daily 9am–5pm; admission fee) with many items that were a bequest from a philanthropist once resident in the house, Palazzo Falson was begun in 1283. Following the expulsion of the Jewish population from Malta in 1492, the synagogue that stood next to the house was disused and was bought by the Falson family. The present house was built in 1495, using the extra space. The stone walls and inner courtyard have changed little since that time. Paintings, furniture and other everyday articles demonstrate a family life played out over the centuries.

A little way beyond Palazzo Falson are the walls of the citadel at **Bastion Square**, offering fine views across nearby valleys towards Mosta. You can walk around the walls here, or visit the cafés. Make your way round to Magazines Street where you will find the **Greek Gate**, a less used entrance

In St Paul's grotto

to the city than the main gate, but a considerably older one. Part of the bastion dates from the period of Arab rule.

Rabat

Beyond the walls of Mdina, **Rabat** could not be more of a contrast. Rabat (an Arab word meaning village) began to grow outside Mdina's walls as a residential suburb that would serve the city during the period of Arab rule. Today, with no Arab traces, it is an untidy town with narrow streets. Dominating its centre is the parish **church of St Paul** (1691) with a **grotto** beneath that is said to have miraculous powers and is consequently a place of pilgrimage. Legend has it that St Paul lived here for three months in stark simplicity. In 1748, to honour the saint, Grand Master Pinto donated the statue of the saint that stands there. Pope John Paul II visited the grotto in May 1990. Also on the parish square is the **Wignacourt College Museum**, a charming old palazzo with a varied collection of paintings and documents.

A short distance away are the Catacombs of St Cataldus, St Paul and St Agatha. These macabre underground burial places were dug into the stone by early Christians who, in times of religious intolerance, often also conducted their religious services in the chambers. **St Cataldus** was dug at the end of the 2nd century while **St Paul's Catacombs** (open daily 9am–5pm; closed public holidays; admission fee) were built after AD400. More than 1000 people were buried here.

St Agatha's Catacombs are reached through a crypt. It has chambers decorated with frescoes dating from the 12th century and a charming small museum.

Just outside the walls of Mdina near the Greek Gate is one of the few remains of the islands' Roman period, a villa believed to have belonged to a wealthy merchant. Reconstructed from the foundations up, it is now the **Domus Romana**, a museum of Roman Antiquities (open daily 9am–5pm; admission fee), with a few interesting mosaics and a collection of Roman objects found here and elsewhere in Malta, including marble statues and busts, terracotta ornaments, glassware and pottery, and some amphorae.

Mosta

Only 3km (2 miles) northeast of Mdina is **Mosta**, a town whose major attraction can clearly be seen from the walls of the old capital. The **Rotunda** of the **church of Santa Maria Assunta** (open daily 9am–noon, 3–5pm and for services after 5pm; free) is said to have the fourth largest dome in Europe and is a masterpiece of design and building skills, as it was completed without the aid of interior scaffolding. The church was designed by George Grognet de Vasse, a Maltese engineer of French origin, and is based on the Pantheon in Rome. Its 51m (167ft) high dome is

Santa Maria Assunta in Mosta

Neolithic grooves in the limestone at Clapham Junction

45m (147ft) in diameter with walls 6m (19ft) thick. During World War II, a German bomb pierced the dome and fell into the church below. The fact that it did not explode was attributed by worshippers to the intervention of the Virgin Mary. A replica of the bomb is on display in the sacristy.

As well as visiting the church, it's worth taking time to explore Mosta's medieval alleys and streets.

Victoria Lines

To the southwest of Mosta and Mdina, Malta becomes more rural, with only a few farming settlements surrounded by terraced fields and joined by bumpy roads. You will see vestiges of old fortifications, including a defensive wall running across the centre of the island, originally built by the British during the Victorian period to protect the south of the island should it be attacked from the north. The **Victoria Lines**, as they are known, became something of a white elephant as warfare changed in the 20th century. Onwards towards the village of **Mġarr** are more Neolithic remains at **Ta' Ħaġrat** and **Skorba**. These are not generally open to the public but you should ask at the tourist information office if you would like to tour them.

Buskett Gardens

South of Rabat, the main road leads down towards the coast. **Verdala Castle** is on this road. The castle was originally a summer residence for Grand Master de Verdale. Designed by Gerolamo Cassar in 1586, the building was designed to look like a fortified castle – complete with dry moat – even though it was not meant to withstand an attack. Today the castle is the summer residence of the president and only rarely open to the public. The extensive gardens are split into two sections, those which form the private gardens of the palace, and an area of natural woodland beyond, known as the *Boschetto* or **Buskett Gardens**, once alive with game for hunting and now a favourite picnic place for Maltese families at weekends during the summer. A large horticultural show is held here each year on 29 June, the feast day of Saints Peter and Paul.

Clapham Junction

South of Buskett are the curious remains called Clapham Junction after the railway junction in south London. These are some of the best examples of the Neolithic grooves in the limestone rock thought to have been made by the temple builders in the 4th millennium BC. The theory goes that these ancient peoples quarried rock from nearby sites and dragged the large megaliths on primitive carts to their religious sites. Over time their regular routes were marked by deep tracks. No one has yet proved this theory correct, but in any case, Clapham Junction is lined with several sets of deep ruts.

The road from Rabat stops abruptly at **Dingli Cliffs**, named after a nearby village. The precipitous drops along much of the south coast are awe-inspiring and are at their most spectacular around Dingli. There are several walking trails in the area; east to the pretty, secluded cove of **Għar Lapsi**, or west to the highest point on Malta at 250m (820ft) above sea level, marked by the **Madalena Chapel**.

THE NORTHWEST

The northwest of Malta has traditionally been less populated than the southeast. In this region you'll find much more farming, much more open space, and resorts that are different in character to the Sliema–St Julians area. At the furthest point is **Ċirkewwa**, with its regular ferry service to Gozo and day-trip boats to Comino.

At **Baħar iċ-Ċagħaq** you will find two attractions to thrill the children. A water park with slides, pools and fair rides is open during the summer (April–October), and next door to it is **Mediterraneo Marine Park**, with fun-loving sea lions and playful dolphins that perform twice daily in the summer months. The Marine Park also operates education programmes, which involve getting behind the scenes with the animal trainers and park workers who keep the animals healthy and happy. These are open to the public and last for 90 minutes.

Qawra

The road continues round the coast to **Salina Bay**, named for the salt flats which have been used for centuries to produce this most important of minerals. Salina Bay marks the start of the second major area developed for tourists, which stretches around the headland of Qawra. This area is characterised by more self-catering accommodation and fewer

St Paul's Island

large hotels than there in Sliema/St Julians. The nightlife is a little more raucous and a little less sophisticated. Having said that, there are more that enough bars, clubs and eateries to satisfy the thousands who enjoy coming here every year.

Buġibba and St Paul's Bay

As you travel further round the headland, **Qawra** melds into **Buġibba** (Boo-jib-ba), a modern town overlooking the waters of **St Paul's Bay**. On the far side of the bay is St Paul's Island, where the saint is believed to have been shipwrecked. His statue dominates the barren rock. Both Buġibba and Qawra have a wide selection of hotels and self-catering apartments, and from the Buġibba waterfront day-trip boats take visitors north to Gozo and Comino or south to Valletta. Just inland from Buġibba, in the small town of **Burmarrad**, is the simple church of **San Pawl Milqi** (St Paul Welcomed), said to be the site where he first preached to the Maltese people.

Għajn Tuffieħa

Two of the islands' most picturesque sandy beaches are **Għajn Tuffieħa** (ayn tuff-eer-ha) and **Golden Bay**, set among dramatic cliffs and separated by a tiny tower that was once a watchtower of the Knights. Golden Bay is the larger of the two, with a car park by its extensive beach facilities at the water's edge. Għajn Tuffieħa can be reached only by a climb down a long stretch of steps or down a rough path, so even in the height of summer it is the less crowded of the two. Għajn Tuffieħa has only a small café to offer refreshment. Both beaches are ideal for children.

Not far from these two bays, at the crossroads leading into the first car park, is a signpost to the village of **Mġarr** and to Ġnejna Bay. Mġarr is a small village with a tall church dedicated to Santa Marija, and a farming community. (The church is known as the Egg Church because the villagers financed the church by donating money generated by selling eggs.) Drive through the village (or proceed on foot as buses do not go further) and the road wanders through the countryside before dipping down into a long fertile valley at the end of which there is another sandy beach, **Ġnejna Bay**. The sand here is a little coarse but it is an unsophisticated beach in yet another picturesque setting, with simple but pleasant facilities. To one side is a ribbon of boathouses cut into the rock, used by families for picnics in the summer.

The main road around St Paul's Bay begins to climb up away from the coast, cutting across the verdant **Mistra Valley**, with its tiny beach. At the top of the hill is a turning to **Selmun**, with its Knights' Palace on the hill, now a hotel. At the crest of the hill, overlooking the bay, is **Mellieħa**, once a remote defensive settlement but now a busy destination. Signs here also lead to **Anchor Bay**, a beautiful natural cove, great for diving and swimming. Here you will also find **Popeye Village**, originally built in 1980 as a set for the

Għadira beach in Mellieħa Bay

film *Popeye* starring Robin Williams. It's a fun place for children to explore and has an amusement park.

Mellieħa Bay

Mellieħa Bay tends to get busy in the summer because it has **Għadira**, arguably the best sandy beach on Malta. There are plenty of facilities here if you want to stay for the day, or you could bring a picnic. Behind the beach is a protected area of wetland known as the **Għadira Nature Reserve** (*ghadira* – pronounced add-eer-ra – means lake), an important haven for breeding birds, both native and migratory. It is open to the public in the mornings except during the breeding season.

From Mellieħa Bay it's only a short ride up and over **Marfa Ridge** to **Ċirkewwa** and the short ferry crossing to Gozo. Boats also take visitors from the quay for day trips to Comino and the Blue Lagoon. At the top of Marfa Ridge there are junctions with secondary roads that lead both left and

The Red Tower

right along the ridge. Both offer excellent panoramic views of Malta and across to Comino and Gozo. On your left on the hill's crest you'll see the **Red Tower** 50m (55yds) from the main road, constructed in 1647; it acted as a communications post with the Knights' garrison on Gozo. To your right are Armier and Little Armier, two small sandy beaches ideal for young families.

Views across the Comino Channel are beautiful, with the domes of the churches of Gozo clearly visible on the skyline across the straits. Maltese families have small chalets by the sea here where they come to enjoy summer weekends.

GOZO

Gozo (Ghawdex to the Maltese) is Malta's smaller sibling, and at 67 sq km (26 sq miles), is less than a quarter of the size. Its history mirrors that of its neighbour yet it has a different character. Life moves more slowly here and seems less affected by tourism. Gozo has far fewer visitors – there are fewer than 10 major hotels here – and much more land is given over to farming. It is hillier than Malta, and is much greener. Gozo still retains more of its traditional lifestyle and this is what makes the island such a pleasure to visit. It is great for cycling and hiking, and it also has some of the Mediterranean's best dive sites.

One thing that you will notice immediately is the lack of concrete buildings on the island. Of course Gozo is not immune to development but most new buildings are constructed of sandstone (the same stone used in the numerous forts and towers), which weathers beautifully and looks wonderful in the mellowing sunlight. Many Gozitans (as the people of Gozo are called) emigrated in the years after World War II and some are now returning to enjoy their old age in the place of their birth. You will see houses with names such as Waltzing Matilda or Stars and Stripes – a sure sign of fond memories of adopted countries far away.

Mġarr

Your first real view of Gozo will be the port of **Mġarr** (Im-jar) whose buildings extend down a hillside and around a small creek. The commercial ferry port with its fishing boats is more functional than pretty. There is a tourist information office and a bank here, along with a couple of cafés

Mġarr harbour, with Għajnsielem, right, and its parish church

St John the Baptist in Xewkija

and the ferry terminal. Beyond the ferry port is a delightful fishing harbour that doubles as a yacht harbour in the season. There are some excellent restaurants here, too, with fresh fish on the menu daily.

Clearly visible from the ferry as it enters the port is the **church of Our Lady of Lourdes**, perched above the harbour. From the parvis there are excellent views of the channel.

You have to climb up and out of the harbour to make it anywhere on Gozo. For cyclists this is an early challenge. All bus routes from the harbour go to Victoria, Gozo's capital. On the way there, just up from the harbour, the road passes through the village of **Għajnsielem**. In the central square is a monument to one Anglu Grech, a local farmer, who, according to tradition, had a vision from the Blessed Virgin Mary requesting him to build a church here. The resulting **church of Our Lady of Loreto** was completed in 1820. Għajnsielem is also the location of the **Gozo Heritage** attraction. Here, with the aid of a series of specially lit tableaux and a special soundtrack, you can journey through the history of the island.

Nearby at **Xewkija** (Shew-kiya) there is a beautiful church. Its dome, which can be viewed quite easily from the main road, is larger than the dome in Mosta, reputedly making it the third-largest unsupported dome in Europe. Dedicated to **St John the Baptist**, the rotunda was built as a replacement for an older church on the site. It was made possible thanks to donations from local people; although begun in 1951, the church was not consecrated for more than 25 years.

Victoria

Situated at the heart of the island, **Victoria** is the administrative, business and social hub of Gozo. The town has only been called Victoria since 1897, when it was renamed by the British in honour of Queen Victoria's silver jubilee. You'll find that Gozitans will refer to it as **Rabat**, its original name.

The main thoroughfare through town, Republic Street, leads to **It-Tokk Square** (now officially known as Independence Square) with its cafés and daily morning market. At the west end of the square is the tourist information office, housed in a circular building dating from 1733, which was the **Banco Guiratale**. The old town, just off of It-Tokk, is a maze of narrow alleys where you can find ladies making lace in the shade of their doorways. There are also numerous craft and antique shops, and a special quarter for old metal kitchenware and other collectibles. Alongside It-Tokk is St George's Square where you will find the Basilica of St George. Built between 1672 and 1678, and badly damaged in the earthquake in 1693, it is richly decorated, with ceilings painted by the Italian artist Giovanni Battista Conti. The ornate wooden statue of the patron saint was carved in 1841.

Saints and fiestas

Victoria is made up of two parishes: St George and St Mary's. There is a keen rivalry between the two as they vie to throw the best festas with the loudest, most spectacular fireworks. Even their band clubs compete, presenting Verdi and Puccini operas with international singers in the principal roles.

This is carried through the streets on the patron saint's day (the third Sunday in July). A painting by Mattia Preti over the choir altar depicts the knight poised at the moment of his victory over the dragon.

The Citadel

Dominating the capital, perched on the top of the high ground below which the city has developed, is the **Citadel**. This one at Victoria is much smaller than Mdina's, but was created at the same time, in the 8th century, when Arab rulers built the imposing defensive walls. The whole settlement suffered badly during Ottoman raids in 1551 and in the earthquake of 1693. Although the church and a number of administrative buildings were rebuilt, much of the Citadel still lies in ruins. The tiny community has a peaceful yet profound atmosphere, especially if you find it empty (try to see it early in the morning or after sunset). The most imposing building is **St Mary's Cathedral**, erected soon after the earthquake and designed by Lorenzo Gafà, who also designed St Paul's in Mdina. Unfortunately there was not enough money available to finish the cathedral and a proposed dome was never erected. However, in 1739 the Italian artist Antonio

The Citadel wall and Cathedral

Manuele was commissioned to paint a marvellous *trompe l'oeil* on the ceiling of the church, creating the wonderfully realistic effect of a dome when viewed from the church's nave. **The Cathedral Museum** is accessed through a door at the side of the building. Here you will find gold and silver items that comprise the cathedral treasury, along with vestments, prayer books and other items. St Mary's feast day is the Assumption, on 15 August, when the statue of Our Lady is carried through the Citadel's crowded streets.

Fresco on the wall of a street in the Citadel

The square in front of the Cathedral is flanked by two important administrative buildings. On the left are the old **Law Courts** (rebuilt in 1687) which link with the Governor's Place (rebuilt early 1600s). Look for the shield of Grand Master Wignacourt on the façade; he was head of the Order when this building opened.

The arch to your left leads to Bondi's Palace, once the meeting place of the Gozo commune or council. The building dates from the 16th century and now houses **Gozo Archaeological Museum** (open daily 9am–5pm; closed public holidays; admission fee). The museum has an excellent collection of artefacts from many eras of the islands' history, including a number of female figurines found at the Neolithic sites. Nearby is a craft area, and you can climb on to the bastions from stone stairs to the right of the museum. To the left you can see the original main gate to the Citadel.

A number of old houses in the Citadel have been restored in recent years. The finest is the **Folklore Museum** (open daily 9am–5pm; closed public holidays; admission fee), on Milite Bernardo Street, right of the Cathedral. The exhibits explain the traditional lifestyle of Gozitans, with original farm machinery, weaving looms, and lace-making paraphernalia. The building itself is also fascinating, with stone staircases, narrow corridors and cool stone walls. Look out also for the **Natural History Museum**, with its collection of rocks and fossils. The **Armoury** (once the Citadel's granary) has a collection of old armaments on display.

The countryside of Gozo offers many attractions, and acres of natural beauty. West of Victoria is the traditional village of **Għarb** (the name means west in Arabic and is pronounced Arb) but before you reach the village, turn off left towards the village of **San Lawrenz**. At this junction is the workshop of **Gozo Glass**. The craftsmen work every day, so you can watch pieces being blown, as pigment is added to produce their characteristic vivid hues. The parish church at San Lawrenz has a dome painted a warm red colour, reminiscent of Italian and Greek settlements.

Dwejra

The main road leads on towards the coastline. Just beyond Gozo Glass on the left is **Ta'Dbeigi Craft Village** where you can see lace being made or pottery being painted. Your final destination is **Dwejra** on the west coast, where there are three remarkable natural attractions.

In a dramatic landscape caused centuries ago by a series of geological faults, the most spectacular sight of all is probably the **Azure Window** (open daylight hours; free), a giant stone archway that stands with one foot in the deep, dark-blue sea. Nearby is the **Inland Sea**, a crater filled by sea that pours in through a concealed fissure in the rocky hillside.

Small craft are moored here and there are simple boat-houses and a café. Although it is possible to swim, most visitors take a boat trip through the narrow tunnel to the dark-blue sea outside for spectacular views of the Azure Window and the towering cliffs that edge this coastline (bargain with the boatman first). Around the Azure Window are some excellent dive sites.

In the bay on the far left, below a watchtower built by the Knights in 1561 to guard the coastline, is **Dwejra Bay** with **Fungus Rock** standing upright at its entrance. In the times of the Knights this tall

The Azure Window at Dwejra

rock was reputed to have a rare medicinal plant growing on its top, so a sentry was stationed on the mainland to prevent poachers. It has been proved that the plant is a fungus with no known medicinal powers.

Ta'Pinu

Travelling back along the main road to Victoria you will see a turning to the national shrine of **Ta'Pinu** on your left. This spectacular church is, like St John's at Xewkija, a relatively young building, consecrated in 1931, but it was built on the site of a much older chapel from the 16th century. Ta'Pinu has a fascinating story. In 1883 Carmela Grima, a local woman, came to the old chapel. She heard a voice telling her

A *frejgatina* in the harbour at Marsalforn

to pray, yet she was alone in the building. A friend confided that he too had heard the voice, and together they prayed for his critically ill mother, who recovered. Following this, several people who came to pray here claimed miracle cures, and gradually the church became a place of pilgrimage. In 1920 work started on this larger church to accommodate the increasing number of devotees visiting Ta'Pinu. The original chapel has been incorporated behind the main altar. In a narrow corridor to the side are crutches, splints and baby clothes, bearing witness to apparent miracle cures after prayer here. Beyond Ta'Pinu across the valley you will see the lighthouse at **Ġordan**, set on a mound offering fine views of the west of the island.

Marsalforn

On the coast north from Victoria is **Marsalforn**, the most developed resort on the island. The collection of small hotels and bars around the narrow bay is lively in summer, although not to the extent of the resorts on Malta. There is a promenade around the bay where local families come to stroll in the sea air, escaping the heat of their inland village streets.

Xlendi

South of Victoria, the coast has only one settlement: the beautiful site of **Xlendi** (Shlen-dee), set in a narrow *wied*, or valley, with a sheltered harbour and fleet of small fishing boats bobbing on the calm water. The tiny community has swelled in recent years and modern sandstone apartment blocks now fill the valley, but this has not yet spoiled Xlendi's beauty. There are several fine restaurants here, making it a favourite place for lunch or dinner. You can then sit and admire the view or take to the hills along the footpaths radiating out along the cliff sides.

Further east along the cliffs is **Ta'Ċenċ** (Ta-chench) which has a superb five-star hotel and numerous fine houses. The land here has ancient dolmen and burial mounds and cart ruts to explore. At the water's edge is **Mġarr Ix-Xini** (Im-jar-ish eeni), with a charming pebbled beach and tiny fish restaurant. The valley is set in a dramatic rural landscape.

The rocks of Ġgantija Temple

Ġgantija

Northeast of Victoria is the town of **Xagħra** (Sha-ra), set on one of the typical hills which dot the Gozitan landscape. There are good views of the surrounding area, which may be one of the reasons why it was chosen as the site of a temple during

Neolithic times. On its outskirts is **Ġgantija** (open daily 9am–5pm; closed public holidays; admission fee), the earliest of the four major temple complexes found in Malta.

Ġgantija means giant woman, and the huge stones of these two temples are said to have been set in place by her around 3500BC. The site was excavated in the 1820s, and a range of statuary and pottery was discovered which is now displayed in the archaeology museums in Victoria and Valletta. The structure was revealed to be an inner wall of limestone and an outer wall of coralline, a harder rock. Each unit has two pairs of apses. In the inner apse there is a niche with a stone altar. The two temples have a common forecourt where it is thought the congregation would have gathered for worship.

Xaghra has other attractions to offer. It is situated on top of a porous limestone ridge and the whole area is cut with caves and ancient underground watercourses, two of which are open to the public. Both **Ninu's Cave** and **Xerri's Cave** offer stalactites and stalagmites and both lie under family homes. You will have a family member as a guide to take you down narrow steps into the caves beneath.

Peaceful coves

East of Ramla Bay there are some beautiful, peaceful coves. Both San Blas Bay and Daħlet Qorrot take a little effort to reach but they are well signposted. San Blas is the island's prettiest sandy beach, reached along the hillside path. Daħlet Qorrot has a much smaller sand strip ringed with boathouses.

Ramla Bay

Beyond Xaghra, on the north east coast is **Ramla Bay**, the only wide sandy beach on Gozo – in fact *ramla* means sand in Maltese. Not surprisingly, it can become busy. You can explore the remains of a small Roman structure just off the beach, and there are footpaths in the hills around. One path leads to

Calypso's Cave, said to be the site in Homer's *Odyssey* where Ulysses was held captive by the nymph Calypso. The walk up to the cave is easy and the views impressive, but you will find the fabled cave disappointing.

The high ground in this part of Gozo is topped by the fast-growing town of **Nadur**, known for its Carnival parade on the Sunday

The sands of Ramla Bay

before Lent when local people dress in grotesque masks and generally make mischief. Many of the newer houses here have been built for expatriates from countries around the world. They spare no expense in creating the most beautiful façades; the ornate balconies and columns are a fitting continuation of traditional Gozitan building techniques.

COMINO

The nearest most people get to tiny **Comino** (2.7 sq km/1 sq mile in total) is gazing at it from the deck of the ferry to Gozo. The island has a permanent population of only six, no vehicles are permitted, and there is just one small hotel. Comino is thus a great place to get away from it all – for walking and relaxing. The most famous attraction of the island is a magnet for divers and boaters. The **Blue Lagoon** is a shallow harbour area with a sandy bottom. The light reflected through the water gives it a brilliant azure colour (you can catch a fleeting glimpse of it from the ferry) that is reminiscent of the Caribbean. Boat trips are available from Valletta or many resorts on the northern coast of Malta.

WHAT TO DO

SHOPPING

Malta has always been a trading island and merchants have always played an important part in its economy. Over the centuries, a number of traditional handicrafts have developed that now form the basis of the typical souvenirs you may want to bring home with you.

Where to Shop

Malta is a great place for browsers. There are no major shopping malls and only a small number of shopping complexes in Sliema and Valletta where many major brands or chains have local branches, including Marks & Spencer and Benetton. In contrast, the narrow streets of Valletta, Rabat and Victoria have a wealth of smaller shops.

Markets are also very popular and there is a regular timetable for every town. The major markets in Valletta are the clothing market on Merchants Street and the huge Sunday morning flea market at St James' Ditch. Most markets sell everything from fresh fruit and vegetables to collectibles, and even pets. Markets take place in the mornings; often the stallholders will have packed away by noon.

There are also two craft centres for you to explore. Here you can not only buy goods, but also see the craftspeople at work. Ta'Qali Village on Malta is situated near Mdina, and on Gozo you will find the craft centre at Ta'Dbiegi, outside the village of San Lawrenz, on the road to the Azure Window.

If you are just looking for inexpensive knick-knacks or T-shirts, you'll find shops in abundance all across the islands.

Sailing dinghies at St Paul's Bay

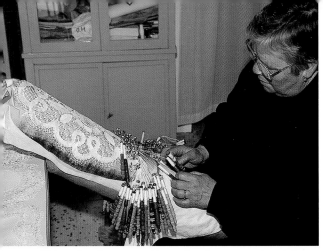

Maltese lace is renowned but only a few women, mostly in Gozo, still practise the fine art

What to Buy

Lace. Only a few years ago it was common to see the women of every village sitting out on their doorsteps making lace. Today, this remarkable handicraft is becoming rare – with few young women interested in learning the skill and cheap machine-produced lace flooding the market. On Gozo you will have a greater chance of finding women lace-making, but you will be able to buy items on Malta. The prices for fine hand-produced lace are reasonable and the quality is superb. You can buy anything from a small handkerchief to bed linen or table linen, and in a variety of colours and patterns.

Sweaters and rugs. Knitted, woven and crocheted goods are also abundant, and offer value for money. Women often sit out on summer evenings with knitting needles or crochet hooks working on items. Sweaters are popular – very useful on those cooler winter days – and come in sizes to fit everyone from the smallest baby to the largest man. Woven rugs are another good practical buy. Made of wool or cotton, they are machine washable, easy to pack, and you will find numerous examples in Maltese family homes.

Silver and gold. Maltese artisans have been creating silver items for generations. You can find picture frames, spoons and christening mugs. The Maltese Cross is of course very popular, as a brooch or on a chain, and is an appropriate souvenir of your time here. Gold is also popular, as can be seen in the shops on St Lucia Street in Valletta.

Glass. On both Malta and Gozo you'll find handmade glass. The distinctive bright colours that swirl within each piece are introduced by adding powdered pigments when the glass is in its molten state. The range of items on offer includes vases, bowls and perfume bottles. The colours of the glass reflect the dominant hues of the islands: the blues and aquas of the sea, verdant greens of the spring landscape, and the beiges of the sand and rocks in the summer sun. Mdina Glass can be found at the Ta'Qali Craft Centre, Malta. On Gozo, Gozo Glass has its studio near Gharb on the main road of the village.

Pottery. It has been produced here since the earliest times – witness the artifacts in the archaeological museums of each island which date from thousands of years BC, from Megalithic statuary to Roman amphora. Modern potters use both traditional and modern designs and you can buy pieces with a range of glazes.

Traditional pottery

Edibles. One theory about the origin of Malta's name is that it came from *melita*, the Greek word for honey. It indicates how important this was to the islands in ancient times. Today honey is used to sweeten a range of Maltese dishes and you can buy pots of it to take home.

Cheese is one of the major products, particularly on Gozo, where it is still hand-produced on small farms. The small rounds of sheep's milk cheese called ġbejniet (j-bay-niet) are excellent and are served fresh, covered in herbs or pepper, or preserved in olive oil with sun-dried tomatoes.

Malta also produces oil and an unusual alcoholic liqueur. Bajtra is made from the juice of the prickly pear, which imparts a purple hue to the liquid. The juice is flavoured with herbs and honey, and the resulting drink is sweetly unique.

ENTERTAINMENT

Pubs and Clubs

Malta has quite a sophisticated range of nightlife for such a small island. This centres on the resort areas of St Julians, Paceville and Buġibba, where the large hotels and self-cater-

Casinos

Malta has three casinos, offering a full range of gambling opportunities. There's the Dragonara Casino alongside the Westin Dragona hotel in St Julians, which is set in a huge Greek Revival-style building, built at the beginning of the 20th century as a summer residence of a local marquis; the Oracle Casino at the New Dolmen Hotel in Qawra; and the Casino de Venezia which overlooks the Cottonera yacht marina at Vittoriosa and is owned by Venice's casino. The casinos open at noon and foreign nationals must be over 18 to enter. Dress code: smart casual.

Nightlife in Paceville

ing apartment blocks have been built. There are numerous bars and English-style pubs, along with an increasing number of wine bars. Many of these have live music or, at the very least, are equipped with superior sound systems. Later in the evening you can head out to a club – there are many to choose from, each changing its identity every year – but be prepared to take your place in a queue at many establishments because the local Maltese jet-set also head out late at night, particularly at weekends. Most of the large hotels also have a schedule of entertainment, from dinner-dances to folklore programmes.

Theatre and Music

Malta enjoys a healthy amount of theatre, ballet and concert recitals, particularly in the winter months. These are centred on venues in Valletta such as the Manoel Theatre and the St James Cavalier Centre of Creativity, and take place at lunchtime as well as in the evening. The website of the Malta Tourist Authority <www.visitmalta.com> has a full list of activities taking place each month, with contact details should you be interested in buying tickets.

OUTDOOR PURSUITS

There are only a few sandy beaches on the Maltese islands, whose coastlines are characterised by rocky stretches and narrow inlets. However, Malta is still popular with those who want to relax by spending time out in the sun. Lido pools with sunning areas are cut into the rocks, providing seawater swimming pools in summer. Should you want to join the smart set, the Reef Club, St Julians, near the Dragonara Casino, is considered the most fashionable and best-appointed lido. Many large hotels will have two or three pool areas with sun decks, which take the place of the beach.

Maltese-style sunbathing

The number of sandy beaches may be limited but there are endless numbers of places where you can swim or snorkel off the smooth rock coastline. A point to remember is that if you see a Maltese or Gozitan family picnicking and swimming along the shore, then that is a good place to swim.

Best Beaches

The largest beaches on Malta are **Mellieħa Bay**, **Għajn Tuffieħa**, **Golden Bay**, **Għadira** and **Ġnejna**, but just as much fun are the smaller places such as **Par-**

adise Bay, **Armier** and **Little Armier**. In Gozo try **Ramla** and **San Blas**. For swimming from the rocks, the best spots are around **Sliema**, **St Julians**, **Paceville** and **St Thomas Bay**; and **Delimara** and **Peter's Pool** in the south. In Gozo the best swimming is around **Marsalforn** and **Xlendi** or in tiny coves like **Mġarr ix-Xini**.

Snorkelling and Diving

With so many rocky inlets, it's not surprising that the Maltese islands are a snorkellers' heaven. The sea is clear and the fish plentiful, along with rock-dwelling creatures such as urchins and octopus.

The waters around the islands are some of the clearest in the Mediterranean with visibility between 40m and 50m (130–165ft). This, along with numerous natural features and wrecks to explore, make the islands popular destinations with divers and snorkellers. Among the wartime wrecks are Royal Navy ships and aircraft.

Maltese law requires all divers to be over 14 years of age and have a medical certificate of fitness. Divers who have less than a PADI (Professional Association of Diving Instructors) advanced certificate or equivalent must dive with a certified instructor. Those who wish to dive independently will need a local dive permit. These are issued by the Malta Department of Health, through your local dive centre on Malta or Gozo.

If you wish to learn to dive there is an excellent network of dive centres, which offer training to professional levels. The

The clear waters around the islands are ideal for diving

centres are affiliated with one of the major certifying bodies, with PADI being the most common. The basic qualification, the Open Water certificate, takes five days to complete. On completion this will allow you to dive with an instructor to a depth of 18m (60ft), which opens up many dive sites to you.

For further information contact the Federation of Underwater Activities, PO Box 29, Gzira GZR 10, Malta, tel/fax: 2131 4348; or the Professional Association of Diving Instructors, 61/2 Msida Seafront, Msida.

Other Activities

Most major hotels offer a full range of watersports, including jet skiing, windsurfing, sailing and 'banana rides'. The centres are generally open to non-guests. Many beach lidos have the same facilities.

If you want to take to the water under your own steam, you can hire anything from a kayak to a 10-berth 'gin-palace'. You'll need a skipper's certificate for anything large – or you can hire a crew as part of the package and leave the hard work to them.

Active Pursuits. The islands offer facilities for a surprising number of sports and the climate is conducive to quite strenuous activities, especially in the spring and autumn months. Malta has an extensive regimen of competitive sporting events throughout the year, including cycle races, marathons, biathlons and triathlons.

Tennis. Most large hotels have tennis courts and these are often floodlit. Tennis is a very popular sport in Malta, with several community court complexes in towns and villages. Or contact the Marsa Sports Club, which welcomes temporary members for golf, squash and tennis; tel: 2123 3851.

Walking. The southwest areas of Malta and along the cliffs at Dingli take you to a rural Malta that you might otherwise not see on your visit. Many parts of Gozo have rural tracks where you can walk, and much of the coastline remains unspoiled. There are plans to put signs along pathways and produce walking maps. Until then, simply follow the main farming paths.

Cruises and Tours

Day Cruises. Take a tour of the Grand Harbour or a day cruise around the island with time for swimming and snorkelling. You can depart on a state-of-the-art catamaran, miniature cruise ship, a Turkish *gulet*, or a gaff-rigged schooner (pretend that you're a pirate). Captain Morgan offers the most comprehensive service, with several sizes of craft. They can even offer an underwater safari boat with Perspex keel, which allows you to enjoy the underwater environment without any risk of getting wet. Contact them at Dolphin Court, Tigne Seafront, Sliema, tel: 2346 3333, fax: 2346 3344, <www.captainmorgan.com.mt>.

Land Cruises. Take a four-wheel drive safari to remote places. You'll see vestiges of the Malta of the past and find out just how diverse these islands are. Captain Morgan Cruises offers jeep safaris with an experienced leader. Drivers must be over 25. Gozo Jeep Tours (45 St Lucy Street, St Lucia, Kercem, Gozo, tel: 2156 1817, fax: 2156 6267, <www.gozo.com/jeeptours>) offer tailor-made Jeep tours of the island, either for specific interests or general sightseeing.

CHILDREN

There are lots of attractions for children and they are made very welcome on the islands. Maltese children are treated with indulgence and will often be out late, especially in summer, taking a stroll along the seafront with parents and grandparents, who will stop for a drink at a café or bar.

A boatman waits at the Blue Grotto

The summer sun is strong, so always make sure that children have plenty of sun screen skin protection at all times, even if they are playing in the water, and cover their heads with a hat.

Boat trips are always fun, whether it be across the Grand Harbour, out to the Blue Lagoon or around Gozo. There is a wealth of sea life to look out for as you travel. A short trip into the Blue Grotto (Malta) or to the Inland Sea (Gozo) will

At Popeye Village

fascinate them as they travel deep into the caves and watch the iridescent water shimmering and reflecting on the walls.

Take a *karrozin* ride around Valletta or Mdina. Children will enjoy being the centre of attention as they trot along, and will appreciate being high above the crowds for a better view. Agree the price before setting off on the ride.

The colourful and lively *festas* are perfect for children. There is lots of music, and no one seems to mind how much noise they make. Spectacular firework displays are a highlight, but it's advisable to prepare the little ones for the noise.

Mediterraneo, at Baħar iċ-Ċagħaq, offers up-close interaction with sea lions and dolphins, with feeding and educational programmes.

Popeye Village, near Mellieħa *(see pages 66–7)*, is a great place to explore, and has an amusement park.

The action of 'In Guardia', at Fort St Elmo will fire your child's imagination about the past in a way that museums cannot *(see panel on page 35)*.

Calendar of Events

In summer hardly a weekend passes without a *festa (see panel page 10)* in one of the many towns and villages on the islands, when the local patron saint is celebrated with three nights of processions, band marches and fireworks. Other events include:

Carnival Traditionally held on the weekend before the start of Lent, as a final exuberant festival before the religious fasting days begin. Noisy parades and fancy dress in Valletta, Malta, and in Nadur, Gozo.

Easter On Good Friday evening there are solemn religious processions in many villages marking the last hours of Christ's life. The biggest are in Mosta and Zejtun. On Easter Sunday church bells ring out joyfully.

Mid-May National Folk Singing Festival: open air festival with Maltese and Mediterranean music and dance in Argotti Gardens, Floriana.

Late May International Fireworks Festival: weekend of spectacular fireworks displays over the Grand Harbour.

7 June Sette Giugno, a public holiday commemorating the bread riots of 1919 when starving Maltese took to the streets. A number were shot by the British soldiers.

29 June The feast of St Peter and St Paul, known locally as Mnarija, takes place in Buskett Gardens, Rabat. It is a sort of harvest festival, with local produce on show and families gathering for picnics in anticipation of the folk singing that takes place after dusk.

Late July The Malta Jazz Festival in the Grand Harbour with international jazz musicians.

15 August Santa Marija, to the locals, but officially the Feast of the Assumption, used by many young Maltese as an excuse for a holiday on Gozo. There is a mass exodus, crowding the island.

8 September Victory Day (also the feast of Our Lady of Victories) marks the ending of the Great Siege of 1565. There is a presidential wreath-laying ceremony in Great Siege Square, Valletta.

Sporting events that may take place in Malta include the International Games of the Small States of Europe, Malta Spring Marathon, World Paralympics Swimming Championships, Malta Open Judo Championships.

EATING OUT

Maltese Specialities

Maltese cuisine is essentially Mediterranean, though there are some outside influences. The many protectors who have come and gone have also played their part, leaving behind them their own ingredients and culinary techniques.

The climate is an important influence on Maltese cuisine. The spring season has ample rainfall that helps to ripen the vegetables, including cabbage, cauliflowers, potatoes and onions (potatoes and onions being important exports). There is no rainfall in summer, but a sophisticated irrigation system allows a different range of crops to flourish (tomatoes, aubergines, melons and grapes), and salad crops are harvested throughout most of the year. Thus the Maltese cook has always worked with the seasonal gluts of various fruits and vegetables – even with the advent of freezers for storage, they still prefer to use whatever is fresh and in season.

Maltese dishes traditionally take time to prepare. This is for a number of reasons, but largely because the lack of wood for stoves and fires meant that creat-

Traditional produce

Malta is renowned for its fresh fish

ing a fire with a high heat was a false economy. In fact, until very recently many villages used a communal oven for hot dishes – usually the village bakery – to make more economical use of the fuel. Because of this slow cooking method, many Maltese dishes do not transfer well to a restaurant menu, and this is in part why relatively few restaurants concentrate solely on Maltese food. As the number of tourists began to grow, the Maltese opened restaurants serving what the visitors ate at home, hence the number of 'international' menus to be found here. This is beginning to change and you can now find Maltese dishes on most restaurant menus.

The very basics of Maltese cooking are excellent. Crusty bread is baked fresh every day – every town has a number of small bakeries so that people can buy bread that is still warm. Often the bread is then drizzled with olive oil and rubbed with a tomato and sprinkled with salt, pepper and a few capers. This simple dish, called *hobz biz-zejt* (literally, bread with oil), provides a staple lunch for many farmers and fishermen during their working days, and is often served today as a pre-appetiser in restaurants. Also as an appetiser, *aljotta* (fish soup) is delicious, with its delicate lemony taste.

Cheese has long been produced from sheep's milk. It is mixed with salt and rennet and then dried (in times past this would have been on the roof under a net). Called *ġbejniet*, the cheeses can be young and soft or, as they mature, quite firm. On menus they are referred to as 'cheeselets'. *Ġbejniet* are often preserved with herbs and pepper, or sealed in a layer of olive oil.

The seas provide ample food in the form of fish, crustaceans, octopus and squid, and you'll see what has been freshly caught sitting on ice in the restaurant. Some seafood is weighed before cooking so that you know the price. Mixed smaller fish are served for a set price, and are steamed or fried.

Over the centuries Maltese cooks learned to make use of bountiful fruits and vegetables, so as to make a little meat or other protein go a long way. They preserved meat in sausages flavoured with herbs and garlic, and mixed fish, meat or cheese with a variety of vegetables encased in pastry. *Lampuki* pie, one of the most popular Maltese dishes, is

Rabbit on the Menu

The land has historically provided a limited supply of protein. *Fenek*, or rabbit, is perhaps Malta's national meat and it is prepared in a number of ways. Most often you will find it on restaurant menus slow-cooked in wine and garlic. Another popular method is fried in oil. The favoured cooking method is rabbit stew, with sauce from the pot served with spaghetti for a first course and the rabbit to follow as a main course, served with plenty of wine.

filleted dorado fish mixed with vegetables and wrapped in pastry. *Pastizzi* are hot filo pastry snacks filled with ricotta cheese or a soft dried pea mixture.

Pasta is also widely used. Having travelled across from Sicily, pasta is considered as Maltese as it is Italian and housewives make it fresh several times a week. A favourite is *ravjul* (ravioli) stuffed with cheese or mincemeat.

Snails

When the autumn rains arrive, the islands see an abundance of snails. Many restaurants offer them as an appetiser, cooked in olive oil and garlic. Be sure to mop up any surplus olive oil with your Maltese bread.

When they are not putting ingredients into pastry or pasta cases, Maltese cooks are stuffing them into other items. The Maltese love *braġjoli* or beef olives – thin beef fillets stuffed with mincemeat, an onion and herb mixture, and smothered in an aromatic tomato-based sauce. Octopus *(qarnit)* and squid *(calamari)* are stuffed, as are the abundant peppers, aubergines and marrows. Rice, mincemeat, onions and tomato sauce are widely used when preparing stuffed vegetable dishes. Equally popular is *ross fil-forn* – oven-baked rice with mincemeat and tomato sauce. *Timpana* is an interesting combination of all three influences: a pastry pie filled with pasta – macaroni – and a mixture of mincemeat, onions and tomato sauce.

Sweets and Desserts

Traditional sweets and desserts have a distinctly eastern or Moorish influence and are often served as finger foods rather than in plate-sized portions, because they are so sweet. Try *imqaret*, deep-fried date-filled pastry, or *biskuttini tal-lewz*, macaroons. *Ħelwa tat-Tork* (Turks' sweets) is Malta's version of halva. *Kannoli*, deep-fried pastry stuffed with ricotta cheese, chocolate and candied fruit, originated in Sicily.

International Cuisine

There is a range of different types of cuisine and the quality is of a high standard. Many restaurants take full advantage of the fresh produce of the islands. You are unlikely to be disappointed by the quality of vegetables that accompany many entrée dishes, although the variety may seem limited after a while. Steaks can be found in many restaurants served with various sauces. Veal *(vitello)* is also popular. French *haute cuisine* is available at a few of the more expensive restaurants.

You can eat in hundreds of trattoria-style restaurants offering pasta and pizza in a friendly informal atmosphere. Restaurateurs are increasingly using Maltese ingredients to give a different slant to pizzas – adding Gozitan cheese, for example, or Maltese sausage – and also to pasta, such as serving it with rabbit instead of the usual *Bolognese* (mincemeat and tomato) or *carbonara* (egg, cream and ham) sauces.

A few English pubs still serve pies and fish and chips, although the Maltese and Italian influence has overtaken this colonial vestige. There is also an increasing number of Indian, Chinese and other south-east Asian restaurants, along with the occasional Greek restaurant or sushi bar.

Open-air refreshments, Valletta

Drinks

Coffee is served in a range of Italian styles, especially espresso and cappuccino, and iced coffee is very popular in summer. Fruit juices are excellent and refreshing, especially on long summer days. Most are freshly produced on the premises. The Maltese produce their own soft drink called Kinnie – a sparkling bitter, citrus drink – and a full range of international soft drinks is also available.

Some international beers are brewed locally under licence. The longest established brewery, however, brews Maltese beers. Cisk, pronounced *Chisk*, is the lighter; Hopleaf is equally refreshing but has a slightly heavier, nuttier taste.

Malta produces a range of wines, which have improved greatly over the past 20 years or so. The wineries have invested heavily in new machinery and techniques, taking advice from French and Californian growers. Grapes imported from Italy supplement home-grown varieties. The leading, most expensive wines are produced under the Meridiana label. Marsovin and Delicata are the producers of most wines found in restaurants and supermarkets. Italian and French wines are imported in great variety to supplement the domestic brands.

Beer on tap

For after-dinner drinks, two rather unusual liqueurs are produced on Malta. Bajtra – said to be the favourite after-dinner tipple of the Knights – is made by distilling the juice of the prickly pear, which imparts an interesting purple hue to the finished drink. The second, Tamakari, is a clear, sweet-flavoured liqueur.

Help with the Menu

To help you to order a meal in a restaurant, the list below contains a selection of the words (Maltese, Italian and French) that you are likely to come across on a Maltese menu. Specific local dishes and desserts are described on pages 93–6.

abbacchio, agnello, ħaruf	lamb
aglio, ail, tewm	garlic
anitra, canard	duck
boeuf, manzo	beef
braġoli, bragioli	beef olives
carciofi, qaqoċċ	artichoke
ċerna	grouper fish *(mérou)*
coniglio, lapin, fenek	rabbit
dolce	dessert
espadon, pesce spada	swordfish
fagioli, fagiolini, haricots	beans
formaggio, fromage	cheese
funghi, champignons	mushrooms
ġbejna	Maltese sheep's milk cheese
homard, aragosta	lobster
lampuka	dolphin fish special to Malta
larinġa	orange
melanzana, brinġiel	aubergine, eggplant
patate, pommes de terre	potatoes
pâtes	pasta
pesce, poisson	fish
piselli, petits pois	peas
prosciutto, jambon	ham
salsa	sauce
tonn, tonno, thon	tuna
uove, oeufs	eggs
vongole	clams

HANDY TRAVEL TIPS

An A–Z Summary of Practical Information

A

ACCOMMODATION (see also CAMPING, YOUTH HOSTELS, and the list of RECOMMENDED HOTELS on page 125)

There is a full range of accommodation in Malta, from five-star hotels to a wide choice of self-catering options. All establishments offering accommodation are classified by the Maltese Hotel and Catering Establishments Board (HCEB) against a pre-determined set of criteria conforming to international standards. Standards of service are also rated, from De Luxe (the highest standard), to Gold, to Bronze (the lowest). The website <www.visitmalta.com> is a useful Internet guide to booking.

Hotels. Hotels are classified from one to five stars. Hotels in class one or two may not have rooms with private facilities. Always make enquiries before making a firm booking. Hotels in the higher star ratings will be well-equipped. Prices are normally quoted per person per night. When room rates are quoted, they include continental breakfast. High season, when prices are highest, is from mid-July to the end of September. Low season is from November to the end of March; however prices will rise at Christmas and Easter. Most hotels are available on holiday packages from Europe.

Many hotels offer full board for relatively little extra cost. However, eating out is inexpensive in the islands.

Self-catering options. Self-catering is a popular choice. It can consist of simple studios or apartments in small blocks, apart-hotels which offer some hotel-style accommodation and some units with kitchens, self-catering holiday complexes with restaurants, pools, etc, or renovated farmhouses set out in the countryside – a particular favourite on Gozo. Many of these are several hundred years old but renovated to provide spacious rooms, bathrooms and a pool. Most are set in picturesque locations. For farmhouse rentals on Gozo try Gozo Farmhouses, 3 Triq i-Imġarr, Għajnsielem, Gozo, tel: 2156 1280, fax: 2155 8794, <www.gozofarmhouses.com>.

AIRPORT

Malta International Airport at Gudja serves the whole of the archipelago. Opened in 1992, it is 10km (6 miles) southeast of Valletta. You will find airline ticketing offices, exchange facilities, car rental offices, a chapel, tourist information bureau, and bars and restaurants here. For flight enquiries tel: 5004 3333.

Taxis are available outside the arrivals terminal for the short journey into town; buy a voucher to your destination at a desk inside the terminal and present it to the driver.

B

BICYCLE HIRE

Bicycling is easy and fun, particularly on Gozo with its quieter roads. All-terrain bikes offer the chance to take to the country tracks away from the towns.

BUDGETING FOR YOUR TRIP

Malta and Gozo are inexpensive destinations by European standards with food, excursions and attractions offering good value for money. Here are a few sample prices to help you to budget for your trip.

Car rental: (small vehicle) around €186 per week in August.
Entrance fee for state museums: €1.35.
Commercial attractions: around €7–12 for adults.
Dinner for one without drinks in a moderate restaurant: €19–24.
Room rate for a medium room: €42–60 per person/per night. Full board may be as little as €12 extra.
Horse and buggy tour: €15 for the first 30 minutes.
Island tour by bus: €14 per person.
Harbour boat tour: €14 per person.
Open water dive course: €235 for one accompanied diver; €16 for full equipment rental for the day.

C

CAMPING

There are no organised campsites on any of the islands.

CAR HIRE

Car hire is on par with most other European countries. In August, hiring a small car will cost around €186 per week. A car will free you from the strictures of the bus timetable or tour itinerary, but driving and navigating around the island is a challenge. Collision damage waiver is fairly expensive (around €14 per day) but will be worth it for the peace of mind. Always check with your credit card or domestic insurance provider as you may be insured through your existing policies.

All the major car-hire companies have offices on the island; however, some are run as franchises rather than as main branches. Some have desks at the airport, and it is possible to pick up a car immediately upon arrival. A number of of the larger hire companies offer more competitive rates if you reserve the car from home.

Here are the contact details of the major hire companies.

Avis local head office, tel: 2122 5986, fax: 2123 5754, <www.avis.com.mt>.

Europcar local head office, tel: 2138 8516, fax: 2137 3673, <www.alpinerentacar.com.mt>.

Hertz local head office, tel: 2131 4636, fax: 2133 3153, <www.hertz.com.mt>.

Percius Car Hire Ltd, tel: 2144 2530, fax: 2143 5947, <www.percius.com>.

Thrifty Leasing, tel: 2147 0896, fax: 2149 9221, <www.meli group.com>.

Most companies have age limits between 25 and 70. Your national driving licence will be acceptable. If you rent in Malta there is no problem with taking your car to Gozo on the ferry.

CLIMATE

Malta has a typical Mediterranean climate with hot, dry summers and, generally, mild winters. Even in the winter months days may have long bouts of sunshine. The short spring is characterised by sunny days with cool breezes. By May the rain ceases until October and the temperature begins to rise quickly. In spring, flowers and crops cover the terraced farming areas, but by the end of May the land becomes parched and by the middle of summer it is almost bare. Summer heat can be exacerbated by warm winds from North Africa, but the situation is mitigated by sea breezes, which cool off the coastal areas.

Air temp		J	F	M	A	M	J	J	A	S	O	N	D
Average daily max.	°F	59	60	62	66	71	82	83	84	82	77	69	63
	°C	15	15	16	19	23	27	30	31	28	24	20	17
Average daily min.	°F	49	49	51	54	59	65	70	71	69	63	57	53
	°C	9	9	10	12	15	19	21	22	20	17	14	11

Sea temp	J	F	M	A	M	J	J	A	S	O	N	D
°F	58	58	58	62	65	70	75	76	77	72	67	62
°C	14	14	14	16	18	21	24	26	25	22	19	16

CLOTHING

You'll need swimwear for the beach or pool, but it is not considered acceptable to walk around town in swimwear.

If travelling during the spring or autumn, bring along a couple of extra layers of clothing – warmer trousers and a sweater or jacket for chillier days (it can be breezy early or late in the season) and to wear in the evenings when it can get cooler. In the winter months, a layer of warm clothing is advised, as well as protection against the rain.

In the evenings casual clothes are acceptable in most establishments. However, if you intend to eat at some of the finer restaurants, the code words are 'smart casual', a jacket for men perhaps (ties are rarely required) and 'dressy' ensemble for women is appropriate – enquire about dress code when you book.

If you intend to visit any of the churches around the islands you should make sure that you are appropriately dressed. This means no variations of swimwear, and both sexes must have their shoulders covered. Men take off hats when entering a church.

COMPLAINTS

In the first instance, complaints should be taken up with the establishment concerned. If you are still dissatisfied and if your complaint is with either a hotel or restaurant, approach the Hotel and Catering Establishments Board who license all such businesses; tel: 2124 2919. For all other complaints contact the Malta Tourism Authority, who should be able to direct you to the appropriate body to advise you further.

CRIME AND SAFETY

Malta is relatively crime-free compared to the rest of the world. However, petty crime such as handbag snatching is on the increase in tourist areas and it pays to take precautions against becoming a victim. Put your valuables in the hotel safe if there is one. Don't carry large amounts of cash, and never leave valuables unattended on beaches or visible in your car. Walk only on well-lit streets at night.

If you do become a victim of crime, you should report this to the police immediately.

CUSTOMS AND ENTRY REQUIREMENTS

Entry Requirements. The following nationalities do not need an entry visa for stays of less than three months: all European Union countries, Australia, New Zealand, Canada and the United States.

If you want to extend a trip beyond three months, a written request must be made to the Commissioner of Police, Police Headquarters, Floriana, before the end of the three-month period.

For the first seven years after its 2004 entry into the European Union, Malta is allowed to impose restrictions unilaterally in urgent and exceptional cases where the influx of workers from the EU creates pressure on the local labour market or particular sectors.

Currency restrictions. There is no limit to the amount of foreign currency that can be imported into Malta, provided that large amounts are declared upon arrival.

Customs. The same customs regulations apply in Malta as in the rest of the European Union. Check with a Malta Tourism office if you are in doubt about specific items.

D

DRIVING

Driving can be seen as an adventure or a nightmare, depending on your point of view. It is not for the faint-hearted, but can be very rewarding since you can make your own timetable and visit the major sites when the large tour groups have departed. Points to remember are the general poor driving ability of the nation, and the sheer number of vehicles on the road. Lane discipline is poor; drivers will pull out of junctions in front of you or turn off without using indicators; travelling through red lights is common. Vehicles will often pull out to pass a line of parked cars, totally blocking your side of the road and leaving you with nowhere to go. Vehicles are often in poor condition, resulting in feeble acceleration, noise and belching exhaust fumes.

Road signs for the major attractions are intermittent, and many streets look identical to the visitor, which can make map-reading a challenge. Having said that, Malta is such a small island that you are never lost, you may simply find yourself somewhere you didn't expect to be. There is little to fear about security and most local people are approachable and only too happy to point you in the right direction.

If you are bringing in your own car be sure to remember your driving licence, insurance certificates including Green Card and registration documents. Customs make thorough checks of car documents entering and leaving Malta.

Road Conditions. In Malta you drive on the left and overtake on the right, as in the UK. Roads have not yet been given official classifications but on most maps should appear either red (major road), yellow (secondary road), or white (country road). Road conditions vary widely. The major roads can be good but are prone to subsidence in coastal areas. Minor or country roads can be very poor, with numerous potholes. Roads in white on maps will be dirt tracks. Always drive with caution and be prepared for the unexpected.

Rules and Regulations. There are speed limits of 65kph (40mph) on highways and 40kph (25mph) in urban areas, although many local people drive much faster. You must also always be prepared to travel at much slower speeds on country lanes. Be constantly vigilant of other road users. Drivers and all passengers must use seat belts. Motorcycle riders must wear a crash helmet.

In most towns and villages there are one-way systems, making a direct route through town impossible.

If you are involved in an accident, call the police (tel: 191) and traffic wardens (tel: 2132 0202). Do not move your vehicle until they arrive. Although this causes mayhem for other road users, it is important to obtain a police report to settle any claims that may arise from a traffic incident.

Fuel Costs. Petrol costs around €1.20 per litre for unleaded. Diesel is around half this price, hence the popularity of diesel vehicles. Fuel stations are open Mon–Sat 7am–6pm; closed Sun. All the service stations have automatic pre-paid pumps that take €5 or €10 notes for petrol service after hours.

Parking. There seem to be far more vehicles than parking spaces, especially in the main tourist resorts and the capital. Street parking is permitted unless there are posted restrictions – these include residents-only parking. A yellow line at the roadside means No Parking. Most new larger hotels have parking lots for guests' use but smaller, older hotels may not. Although leaving a car on the street is not a problem as far as security is concerned (don't leave valuables in your car), finding a parking space near your hotel could be.

Parking in Valletta is difficult. There is an underground parking lot near the bus station, and parking along the city wall by Marsamxett Harbour. It is easier to leave the car at one of these places and enter the city on foot.

Most of the major sites outside Valletta have a parking area. These are often manned by unofficial parking attendants wearing peaked hats, who will orchestrate your arrival and departure in exchange for a small sum – carry small change like €2 for this purpose.

Road Signs. Malta uses international road signs, and many will be instantly understandable. Official signs are in English.

If You Need Help. In the event of a breakdown, there are many mechanics on Malta who will tow your vehicle and make on-the-spot repairs at an inexpensive price. However, it is advisable to speak to your car rental agency about who to contact in such an eventuality.

E

ELECTRICITY

The electrical supply is 240 volts/50 cycles and the British style 3-pin, 13-amp socket is standard.

EMBASSIES AND CONSULATES

The following countries have diplomatic representation on Malta:
Australia: Australian High Commission, Ta'Xbiex Terrace, Ta'Xbiex, tel: 2133 8210, fax: 2134 4059, <www.malta.embassy.gov.au>.
New Zealand: Consulate, Villa Hampstead, Oliver Agius Street, Attard, tel: 2143 5025, email: <jill.camilleri@nzcmalta.com>.
United Kingdom: British High Commission, Whitehall Mansions, Ta'Xbiex, tel: 2323 0000, fax: 2323 2234, email: <bhcvalletta@fco.gov.uk>.
US: Embassy, 3rd Floor, Development House, St Anne Street, Floriana, tel: 2561 4000, fax: 2124 3229, <www.valletta.usembassy.gov>.
France: 130 Melita Street, Valletta, tel: 2123 3430, email: <france@global.net.mt>.
Germany: Il-Piazzetta, Tower Road, Sliema, tel: 2133 6531, fax: 2133 3976, email: <info@valletta.diplo.de>.
Italy: 1 Vilhena Street, Floriana, tel: 2123 8157, fax: 2123 3157, email: <ambasciata.lavalletta@esteri.it>.
Libya: Dar il-Jamahariya, Notabile Road, Balzan, tel: 2148 6347, fax: 2148 3939, email: <libyanpeople@waldonet.net.mt>.
Palestine: Villa Kasana, Triq il-Verdun, Kappara, tel: 2138 2355, fax: 2137 0605, email: <jtaweel@onvol.net>.
Tunisia: Valletta Road, Attard, tel: 2141 7070, fax: 2141 3414, email: <at.lavalletta@maltanet.net.mt>.

EMERGENCIES

In an emergency, dial 196 for an ambulance, 199 for fire and crime, 191 for police and 2132 0202 to report traffic accidents.

G

GAY AND LESBIAN TRAVELLERS

Malta is a conservative Catholic country, and same-sex relationships could be shocking for many residents. However, there is a noticeable gay community, and a small number of gay-friendly bars can be found in the tourist resort areas of Paceville and St Julians.

GETTING THERE

By Air

The national carrier for the islands is Air Malta. It operates a comprehensive number of services to Europe and North Africa, and has regular flight connections with the following cities: London Heathrow/Gatwick/Stansted, Glasgow, Birmingham and Manchester in the UK; Dublin and Cork in the Republic of Ireland; Amsterdam, Brussels, Paris, Geneva, Frankfurt and Rome. All of these connections allow for easy onward travel from destinations in the US (Air Malta has partnership agreements with TWA via London Gatwick or Milan Malpensa), Canada, South Africa, Australia and New Zealand. As a guide, the flying time from London is around three hours. Visit <www.airmalta.com> for Air Malta schedules.

Other airlines that operate scheduled services to Malta include: Air France, Alitalia, Austrian Airlines, British Airways, CSE, Emirates, KLM, Lufthansa and Tunisavia. Low-cost airlines include Ryanair and Meridiana.

Gozo has no airport, but a seaplane provides a scheduled service from Valletta's Grand Harbour to Mġarr harbour, Gozo.

Charter flights. Several operators fly to Malta from Europe all year round, with extra flights in summer. These flights can be booked only with hotels/self-catering accommodation as part of the package. The main companies operating from the UK are Air 2000, Air UK, My-Travel and Thomson. As subsidiaries of Air Malta, Belleair Holidays (<www.belleair.co.uk>) and Malta Direct (<www.maltadirect.com>) offer year-round flights and package holidays to the Maltese islands.

By Sea

Malta is linked by ferry services with mainland Italy, Sicily and Tunisia by Grimaldi Ferries (<www.grimaldi-ferries. com>). A weekly service runs from Salerno (near Naples) to Tunis, then on to Malta's Grand Harbour before returning to Salerno. (Malta–Salerno takes 24 hours.) The car ferry has good facilities, cabins and a restaurant.

A much quicker connection, at 90 minutes, is from Pozzallo and Catania (2½ hours) in southern Sicily with a high-speed car/passenger service that sails daily, weather permitting. The service extends to Reggio Calabria, Italy, weekly. It is operated by Virtu Ferries, Malta, tel: 2131 8854/5/6, <www.virtuferries.com>.

A number of cruise lines offer Malta on their Mediterranean itineraries. These include Fred Olsen Lines, Holland America Line, Royal Caribbean, Cunard and P&O.

By Car

If you travel with your own vehicle no bond is required in order to enter Malta, as long as you are planning to stay for less than three months. A Green Card will be necessary – this extends your insurance cover so that your vehicle is covered for third party while you are driving overseas – and can be obtained through your national motoring or touring organisation. Be prepared for customs to finely check your documents and insurance cover as you enter the islands.

By Rail

Rail services connect to the ports of ferries (see above) sailing to Malta from Italy and Sicily (Catania). It is a time consuming way to travel, although Italian trains always run on schedule.

GUIDES AND TOURS

A number of reliable companies offer daily tours around the island or to Gozo. These normally include a guide, but the quality of guides varies. The Malta Tourism Authority licenses a number of guides for itineraries; contact them for more details. Captain Morgan Cruises offer a full programme of tours by air, sea or on land. You can contact them at: Dolphin Court, Tigné Seafront, Sliema, tel:

2134 3373, fax: 2133 2004, <www.captainmorgan.com.mt>. Gozo
Jeep Tours offer tailor-made Jeep tours of the island, catering for
specific interests or just general sightseeing. They can be contacted
at 45 St Lucy Street, St Lucia, Kercem, Gozo, tel: 2156 1817, fax:
2156 6267, <www.gozo.com/jeeptours>.

H

HEALTH AND MEDICAL CARE

Health concerns. There are no serious health concerns to worry
about when you visit Malta. In summer the sun is strong, and even
early or late in the season it is sensible to take precautions against
sunburn. To avoid it, limit your time in the sun during your first
few days, apply sunscreen products regularly, and carry clothing to
cover your skin should it begin to burn. Wear a hat and sunglasses.
Don't forget that the effects of the sun can penetrate water – so you
still need protection in the pool or the sea. Always make sure that
young children are adequately protected while playing. Mosquitoes
can be a problem; always carry insect repellent with you and apply
it regularly if required and especially in the evenings.

The standard of general medical facilities is good and all medical
personnel speak excellent English. There is one general hospital on
Malta and one on Gozo. There are also several health centres open
24 hours a day for minor health problems/accidents. In an emergency dial 196 for medical assistance.

Mater Dei Hospital, Tal-Qroqq, Msida, tel: 2545 0000.

Gozo General Hospital, Għajn Qatet Street, Victoria, tel:
2156 1600.

Vaccinations. No vaccinations are normally needed unless you are
arriving from a cholera or yellow fever-infected area and are within
six days of leaving that area.

Water. Although it is safe to drink the tap water, it does not always
taste pleasant. Bottled mineral water is available everywhere.

Insurance. A comprehensive insurance policy that covers accidents and illness, among other items, is recommended. This will cover the cost of emergency treatment, aftercare or repatriation.

Emergency treatment. Malta has reciprocal health agreements with the EU and Australia. Nationals from these countries will receive free health treatment.

A range of over-the-counter drugs is available to treat everyday ailments, and pharmacists will be able to advise you on minor ailments. Most prescription drugs are available on the islands. A letter from your doctor will be needed for a prescription to be issued by a Maltese doctor. Pharmacists are open during normal store hours and a few also open on Sunday mornings (check the local press).

HITCHHIKING

Hitchhiking is not illegal but it is not common (probably because bus fares are so cheap). Although Malta is a very safe country, hitchhiking has its inherent dangers, and women travelling alone should take great care.

HOLIDAYS

On the public holidays listed below, tourist shops and restaurants will be open, but local shops, supermarkets, offices and banks will all be closed.

Public holidays in Malta and Gozo are:

1 January	New Year's Day
10 February	St Paul's Shipwreck Day
19 March	St Joseph's Day
31 March	Freedom Day
March/April	Good Friday, Easter Sunday and Easter Monday
1 May	Labour Day
7 June	Commemoration of 7 June 1919 *(Sette Guigno)*
29 June	St Peter and St Paul Day *(L'Imanarja)*
15 August	Feast of the Assumption

8 September	Victory Day
21 September	Independence Day
8 December	Feast of the Immaculate Conception
13 December	Republic Day
25 December	Christmas Day

L

LANGUAGE

There are two official languages in Malta: Maltese or *Malti* – the national language, an ancient language that is related to Arabic and written in the Roman script – and English, which is spoken fluently by most of the population.

Many street names and signs in major towns are printed in Malti and English, but not all. So it helps to have a basic understanding of how certain letters and words are pronounced. This will certainly help you when you need to ask someone for directions, although local people will usually go out of their way to make sure that you are heading in the right direction.

ċ	–	like *ch* in *child*
g	–	as in *good*
ġ	–	like *j* in *job*
għ	–	h - silent
h	–	silent, unless at the end of a word (*h* as in *hello*)
ħ	–	*h* as in *have*
j	–	like *y* in *year*; **aj** like *igh* in *high*; **ej** like *ay* in *say*
q	–	almost silent – like a very faint *kh*-sound; a bit like the Cockney glottal stop in 'ain't it'
x	–	like *sh* in *shop*
z	–	*ts*
ż	–	*z*

Common Town and Site Names

The Maltese like to hear at least the names of their towns and villages pronounced properly. So here's a list of the main sites mentioned in this book.

Birżebbuġa	bir-zeb-boo-ja
Borġ in-Nadur	borj in nah-door
Buġibba	boo-jib-ba
Ġgantija	j'gan-tee-ya
Għadira	add-eer-ra
Għajn Tuffieħa	ayn tuff-ee-ha
Għar Dalam	ar da-lam
Għar Lapsi	ar lap-see
Għarb	arb
Ħaġar Qim	ha-jar-keem
Marsamxett	mar-sam-shet
Marsaxlokk	mar-sash-lok
Mdina	im-dee-na
Mellieħa	mel-ear-ha
Mġarr	im-jar
Mnajdra	im-niy-dra
Naxxar	nas-shar
Qala	ar-la
Qawra	ow-ra
Qormi	or-mee
Siġġiewi	sij-jeer-wee
Tarxien	tar-sheen
Xagħra	sha-ra
Xewkija	shew-kiya
Xlendi	shlen-dee
Żebbuġ	zeb-booj
Żejtun	zay-toon

A Few Everyday Expressions

	Maltese	pronunciation
good morning	**bonġu**	bon-joo
good evening	**bonswa**	bon-swa
yes	**iva**	ee-va
no	**le**	le
please	**jekk jogħġbok**	yek yoj-bok
thank you	**grazzi**	grat-see
excuse me	**skużi**	skoo-zee
Where is ...?	**Fejn hu ...?**	fayn oo
right	**lemin**	le meen
left	**xellug**	shel-loog
straight ahead	**dritt il-quddiem**	drit il ood-deem
How much?	**Kemm?**	kemm

Numbers

0	**Xejn**	shayn
1	**Wieħed**	wee-hed
2	**Tnejn**	tnayn
3	**Tlieta**	tl-ear-ta
4	**Erbgħa**	er-ba
5	**Ħamsa**	hum-sa
6	**Sitta**	sit-ta
7	**Sebgħa**	seb-ba
8	**Tmienja**	tmeen-ya
9	**Disgħa**	dis-sa
10	**Għaxra**	arsh ra

LAUNDRY AND DRY CLEANING

All four- and five-star hotels have laundry and dry-cleaning on site. Alternatively, Swan has a number of sites throughout Malta with a free phone number (tel: 0800 776614) for door-to-door delivery.

M

MAPS

The Malta Tourism Authority prints a number of maps and short guides that are perfect for exploring the major towns of the islands on foot. If you require a map that is suitable for touring by car, there is a range available from tourist shops around the islands. None of these maps has comprehensive coverage of the one-way systems in each town or village, but they are helpful for getting from place to place.

MEDIA

Newspapers. The main English-language newspapers for the island are *The Times* and *The Independent*. Both tend to concentrate on local political and domestic issues, covering international news in brief. Most major hotels and newsagents sell the major British dailies on the evenings of the days they are printed. The *International Herald Tribune* is also available, but the major American newspapers are more difficult to find and will be one or two days old.

TV. Most hotels offer a satellite service with CNN and the BBC, German, Italian, French and Arabic channels.

MONEY

Cash. The official currency of Malta and Gozo was the Maltese Lira but on 1 January 2008 changed to the euro, bringing Malta in line with other European Union countries. Notes are denominated in 5, 10, 20, 50, 100 and 500 euros; coins in 1 and 2 euros and 1, 2, 5, 10, 20 and 50 cents.

There is no limit to the amount of foreign currency that can be imported into Malta, provided large sums are declared on arrival. Customs officials have the right to search and question departing passengers with regard to currency on their person.

Currency Exchange. Currency can be exchanged at banks, government accredited currency bureaux, hotels and some shops. Banks offer the best exchange rates.

ATMs and credit cards. A large number of banks have ATMs which accept international debit or credit cards – look for the familiar symbols on the machine. Some machines will impose an extra charge on withdrawals from foreign banks. Credit cards are widely accepted throughout the islands in hotels, shops and restaurants. You will even be able to buy goods from some market stalls with them. An increasing number of businesses can also accept payment by international debit card (Maestro); you will see signs in the window advertising the facility.

Travellers' cheques. Most hotels and many major stores are happy to accept travellers' cheques in payment. You can also cash travellers' cheques at banks and hotels.

OPENING TIMES

Opening hours on the islands, as in many Mediterranean countries, can be complicated. Winter hours are longer than those in summer, when the heat becomes oppressive in the afternoons. Generally speaking, longer working days begin on 1 October and end on 16 June. If you have any important business to attend to, it would be advisable to do it in the mornings when banks, offices, shops and government buildings are definitely open.

All commercial activity stops at lunchtime whatever time of year it is; even the major churches are closed so that the Maltese can observe the tradition of a substantial midday meal followed by an afternoon siesta. The shops generally re-open around 4.30pm and stay open during the week to about 7pm.

Banks. Different banks have slightly varying opening hours, but as a general guide they are open Mon–Fri 8am–12.45pm, Sat

8–11.30am, plus Friday afternoons 2.30–4pm. The main branches open Mon–Fri 4–7pm.

Bars, cafés and restaurants. Bars open in the evenings and, in tourist areas, close around 1am. Cafés open for coffee and snacks around 8am and close between 6pm and 1am. Restaurants open for lunch, generally noon–3pm, and dinner, 7–11pm.

Government offices. From 16 June–30 Sept they are open Mon–Fri 7.30am–1.30pm. From 1 Oct–15 June 7.45am–12.30pm and 1.15pm–5.15pm.

Museums. Museums are generally open Mon–Sat 8.15am–5pm, Sun 8.30am–1pm.

Shops. Mon–Fri 9am–1pm and 4.30pm–7pm, Sat 9am–1pm. Many shops in tourist areas do not close for lunch and are open longer hours, especially in summer. The law forbids Sunday trading except for newsagents.

P

POLICE

The police in Malta are friendly and approachable, and they will certainly offer assistance if you are lost. They wear blue uniforms in the summer, and black (with peaked caps) in winter. Police vehicles are blue and white. Some officers may travel by scooter; these have no official markings.

There are police stations in each major town but not all are staffed 24 hours a day. For a crime emergency tel: 199.

Report traffic accidents to the police and do not move your vehicle until they arrive. To report traffic accidents, tel: 191.

Police headquarters are at St Calcidonius Square, Floriana, Malta, tel: 2122 4001 or 2122 4002.

On Gozo, tel: 2156 2040.

For an ambulance, tel: 196.

In case of fire, tel: 191.

POST OFFICES

Malta has a relatively efficient postal system; usual opening hours are Mon–Sat 7.30am–12.45pm. The post offices at 305 Qormi Road, Qormi, and at the airport are open Mon–Sat 8am–6.30pm.

In Gozo the main office is at 129 Republic Street, Victoria; opening hours are Mon–Sat 7.30am–12.45pm.

Post boxes are distributed in street-side locations and are painted red. They may either be inserted into the wall or round free-standing structures.

PUBLIC TRANSPORT

Buses. The local bus service on Malta is comprehensive, reliable and cheap – a maximum of 93 cents for the longest journey. Some buses are 1960s models, but they are being replaced by more modern vehicles. In Malta they are yellow, in Gozo grey.

In Malta, bus services start from a central hub just outside City Gate in Valletta or on the Sliema harbour waterfront and operate on a fixed schedule. A Malta bus map is available from the travel information kiosk in the bus station. This gives all route numbers and destinations, shows where the bus stop for each number is located in the station, and gives the current fare structure for journeys. Day tickets are available up to a maximum of a seven-day ticket; the price for this is €9.40 per person. The tickets can be bought at terminus kiosks.

Gozo buses have a terminus at Main Gate Street in Victoria. The buses operate on a circular route with no fixed timetable. A service connects with the ferry timetable to allow you to reach Victoria easily on your arrival on the island. Fares are a maximum of 35 cents per person per journey.

Taxis. The white taxis are fitted with meters and should charge the government-controlled rates that should be on display in the cab. If you find that a driver is reluctant to use his meter, agree a price before starting your journey. Many local car hire companies, such as Percius (tel: 2144 2530) and Wembleys (tel: 2137 4141), have chauffeur-driven black Mercedes that are no more expensive than taxis and can be pre-booked. They are also available for all-day hire, for sightseeing.

Ferry. The Marsamxetto Steamferry Service, Dolphin Court, Tigné Sea Front, tel: 2133 1961, fax: 2133 4420 runs a passenger-only service between Sliema and Valletta. The service operates Mon–Sat at a cost of 82 cents one way.

Horse drawn buggies (*karrozin*). These offer tours rather than journeys. Official fares are €7 for 30 minutes and €2 for each subsequent 30 minutes, however these are rarely enforced and a fare should be agreed before you start your journey. You will find them in Valletta, Mdina and Sliema.

Between the islands
Air. There is no direct air link between the islands. A small seaplane flies from the Grand Harbour to Mġarr, Gozo, but does not connect with airline schedules. There is no connection with the airport. It is used by commuters and visitors on excursions.
Sea. The Gozo Channel Company (tel: 2155 6016, <www.gozo channel.com>) operates passenger and light vehicle ferries from Ċirkewwa (on the western tip of Malta) to Mġarr on Gozo. The passenger ferry sails hourly from 5am to 1.30am, but timetables change with each season. Tickets are purchased at Mġarr.

The Comino Hotel has a ferry boat that provides transport to both Malta and Gozo. Seasonal services to Comino also sail from Ċirkewwa and nearby Marfa.

A number of private boats offer tours of Gozo or the Blue Lagoon on Comino from Ċirkewwa or resorts along the northern coastline of Malta. Many of them operate during the summer only.

R

RELIGION

The Maltese population is predominantly Roman Catholic but there are Anglican, Baptist, Buddhist, Jehovah's Witness, Jewish, Methodist, Mormon, Muslim and Orthodox places of worship on Malta.

T

TELEPHONE

The international country code for Malta and Gozo is 356 followed by the number. When making an international call always dial 00 before the country code.

Go is the provider of all land line services in the islands. Most hotels will offer direct-dial long-distance and international phone facilities, but these are priced at a premium and can be extremely expensive. Go has a 24-hour office offering calling, faxing and email facilities at Mercury House, St George's Road, Paceville, tel: 2124 0000.

Phone calls, including international calls, can be made from call boxes and kiosks using coins and credit cards, although newer boxes may only accept cards. Phone cards of various denominations can be purchased from newsagents, post offices and supermarkets.

TIME ZONES

Malta operates on Central European Time (CET), which is one hour ahead of Greenwich Mean Time in winter and two hours ahead between the end of March and the end of October.

In summer the following times apply:

New York	London	**Valletta**	Jo'burg	Sydney	Auckland
6am	11am	**noon**	1pm	10pm	midnight

TIPPING

Tipping for good service is expected in Malta. Some restaurants include a service charge in the final bill but most do not. If no service charge has been included, a tip of 10–12 percent is usual.
The following other guidelines apply:
Taxi driver: no tip.
Porters: 40 cents per piece of luggage.
Chauffeur: €2.
Hairdresser: €2.

TOILETS

Public toilets are to be found in most of the major towns – look for them in market squares, harbours or near bus stations. Standards of cleanliness vary. Malta's museums and historical sites are all striving to provide facilities even if they are in the form of portable toilets. You can use the facilities in bars. If there is an attendant, a small tip is appropriate.

TOURIST INFORMATION

The Malta Tourism Authority (MTA) is responsible for tourist information and it has a number of excellent leaflets and brochures to help visitors make the most of their trip.

The head office of the organisation also acts as a centre for information during your stay on the island: Auberge d'Italie, Merchants Street, Valletta CMR 02, Malta, tel: 2291 5000, fax: 2291 5893, <www.visitmalta.com>.

The MTA also has offices in the following countries:
UK and Ireland: Malta Tourist Office, Malta House, 36 Piccadilly, London W1J 0LD, tel: 020-72924900, <www.visitmalta.com>.
US and Canada: Malta National Tourist Office, Empire State Building, 350 Fifth Avenue, Suite 4412, New York NY 10118, tel: 212-6959520, fax: 212-6958229, <www.visitmalta.com>.

During your stay you may find it useful to visit the local tourist information bureaux at the following addresses on the islands:

Malta: Malta International Airport arrivals lounge, tel: 8007 2222; 1 City Arcades, City Gate, Valletta, tel: 2123 7747.

Gozo: 1 Palm Street, Victoria (in Republic Square), tel: 2156 1419.

TRAFFIC WARDENS

Traffic control and enforcement of parking restrictions are the duties of Local Wardens. Visitors are regarded just as harshly as locals. If you have a dog, a warden will check that you have a pooper-scooper with you. The wardens wear brown uniforms with a yellow reflective sash.

WEBSITES

Websites can be found in the contact details of individual attractions, hotels and restaurants throughout this guide. However, here are a few others that may help you to plan your trip.

www.aboutmalta.com
www.choosemalta.com
www.holiday-malta.com
www.malta.co.uk
www.searchmalta.com

WEIGHTS AND MEASURES

Malta uses the metric system.

YOUTH HOSTELS

The head office of the Youth Hostels Association is:
17 Triq Tal-Borg (Tal-Borg Street), Paola, Malta, tel: 2169 3957.

Recommended Hotels

Malta has a large range of hotels, with a number of fine new five-star establishments complementing hotels of other standards. Choices around the capital are limited since the resort areas have grown around the coastal bays – originally at St Paul's and Bugibba, more recently at St Julians/Sliema.

Prices are reasonable by European standards. The smaller budget hotels may have more limited facilities, but all will be spotlessly clean. Most large hotels will offer prices for B&B, half-board or full board, but with the range and good value of eateries around the island, it would be shame to limit yourself to the hotel restaurant for the whole of your stay.

Prices are generally quoted per person per night with breakfast included. All rooms in three-star establishments and above must have private facilities. Prices rise during the summer months and holiday periods such as Christmas and Easter when it would be wise to make a reservation before you travel.

The symbols below give an indication of peak season prices per person per night, including breakfast.

€€€€€	over 95 euros
€€€€	60–95 euros
€€€	45–60 euros
€€	25–45 euros
€	below 25 euros

MALTA

(The international telephone code for Malta and Gozo is 356)

VALLETTA

Castille €€€ *348 St Paul Street, Valletta VLT 01, tel: 2124 3677, fax: 2124 3679, <www.hotelcastillemalta.com>.* Close to Upper Barrakka Gardens, this hotel is set in a converted 17th-century town house. Some rooms have balconies. Facilities include two restaurants, a coffee shop and a bar. 39 rooms.

Grand Harbour €€ *47 Battery Street, Valletta VLT 01, tel: 2124 6003, fax: 2124 2219.* Small hotel with great harbour views. Rooms are small, clean, and have a TV. Facilities include restaurant and sundeck. 24 rooms.

Osborne €€–€€€ *50 South Street, Valletta VLT 01, tel: 2123 2127, fax: 2124 7299, <www.osbornehotel.com>.* This well-appointed budget hotel is located in the centre of the city. All rooms have A/C and TV. Facilities include a pleasant bar, restaurant and small roof spa pool. 51 rooms.

Phoenicia €€€€€ *The Mall, Floriana VLT 16, tel: 2122 5241, fax: 2123 5254, <www.phoeniciamalta.com>.* This fine building is ideally placed, located only a few minutes' stroll from the centre of Valletta, and from the main bus station for the rest of the island. Facilities include three restaurants, two bars, hairdressers, outdoor pool. 136 rooms.

SLIEMA, ST JULIANS, PACEVILLE

Corinthia Marina €€€€€ *St George's Bay, St Julians STJ 02, tel: 2138 1720, fax: 2138 1708, <www.corinthiahotels.com>.* An attractive hotel with all rooms overlooking the bay. Friendly, well-appointed with a selection of restaurants and cafés. It also shares beach facilities with its elegant neighbour, the Corinthia San Gorg. 189 rooms.

Corinthia San Gorġ €€€€€ *St George's Bay, St Julians STJ 02, tel: 2137 4114–6, fax: 2123 4219, <www.corinthiahotels.com>.* At the entrance to St George's Bay on the water's edge, this member of the Corinthia Group is an ideally placed hotel for enjoying the sea and the sun. Facilities include a wide choice of restaurants, excellent health spa, swimming pools and a popular beach lido. Executive suites. Business Centre. 250 rooms.

Fortina Spa Resort €€€€ *Tigne Sea Front, Sliema SLM 15, tel: 2134 3380, fax: 2346 2162, <www.hotelfortina.com>.* Situated in Marsamxett Harbour with excellent views of the Valletta skyline, the ever-expanding hotel is a few minutes' walk to Sliema's shopping streets and waterfront. An all-inclusive hotel with attractive landscaped gardens, four restaurants, two pools and three spas that offer a variety of health treatments. 220 rooms.

Golden Tulip Vivaldi €€€€ *Dragonara Road, St Julians STJ 06 tel: 2137 8100, fax: 2137 8101, <www.goldentulipvivaldi.com>*. In the heart of Paceville, close to the sea and to Dragonara Casino, this large modern hotel has many rooms with sea views, conference facilities, rooftop pool, fitness centre and a selection of restaurants. 205 rooms.

Hilton Malta €€€€€ *Portomaso, St Julians STJ 02, tel: 2133 6201, fax: 2138 6386, <www.hilton.com>*. This imposing hotel sits on the headland at St Julians. Facilities include five restaurants, three bars, shopping arcade, garden, gym, steam room, squash and tennis courts, indoor and outdoor pools and disco. Wheelchair access throughout. 294 rooms.

Intercontinental Malta €€€€€ *San Wistin Street, St Julians STJ 02, tel: 2137 7600, fax: 2137 2222, <www.malta.intercontinental. com>*. A short distance from the sea, this modern large hotel has six restaurants and cafes, two pools (one at rooftop level), conference facilities and a popular health club. At the heart of the entertainment district. 451 rooms.

Juliani €€€€ *St Julians STJ 06, tel: 2137 6444, <www.hoteljuliani. com>*. Deluxe hotel, small and new overlooking picturesque bay. Rooftop pool. Fashionable restaurants. 44 rooms.

Preluna Hotel and Towers €€€ *124 Tower Road, Sliema SLM 01, tel: 2133 4001, fax: 2134 2292, <www.preluna-hotel.com>*. This large hotel on the main coastal road at the eastern end of Sliema is popular with tour groups. Many rooms have sea views. Facilities include three restaurants, three bars, indoor and outdoor swimming pools (the outdoor pool is across the street), gym, sauna and a variety of watersports, including a scuba diving school. Ramps throughout. 280 rooms.

Radisson SAS Bay Point Resort €€€€€ *St George's Bay, St Julians STJ 02, tel: 2137 4894, fax: 2137 4895, <www.islandhotels.com>.* Situated on the edge of St Julians and Paceville, within easy reach of the nightlife yet removed from it. Facilities include four restaurants, five bars, gym, private beach, sauna, indoor and outdoor swimming pools, tennis courts and powered watersports. All rooms have views of the sea. 252 rooms.

The Waterfront €€€€ *The Seafront, Gzira SLM 03, tel: 2133 3434, fax: 2133 3535, <www.waterfronthotelmalta.com>.* Nicely positioned facing Valletta on the waterfront where daily cruise boats set out. All rooms have a view. Rooftop swimming pool. Two restaurants. Minutes' walk into Sliema.

Westin Dragonara Resort €€€€€ *Dragonara Road, St Julians STJ 02, tel: 2138 1000, fax: 2137 8877, <www.westinmalta. com>.* Stylish family hotel set in landscaped gardens on its own peninsula, close to Dragonara Casino and St Julians entertainment district. Most rooms have sea views. Good restaurants, pools, conference facilities and children's club. 313 rooms including 25 suites and 2 penthouses.

SALINA BAY, ST PAUL'S BAY, MELLIEHA BAY

Coastline Hotel €€€ *Coast Road, Salina Bay SPB 08, tel: 2157 3781, fax: 2158 1104, <www.islandhotels.com>.* Large hotel overlooking Salina Bay, a couple of miles from Buġibba, and popular with tour groups from Europe. Facilities include two restaurants, two bars, large gym, sauna, indoor and outdoor swimming pools, tennis courts. 208 rooms.

Dolmen Resort €€€€ *St Paul's Bay SPB 05, tel: 2158 1510, fax: 2158 1532, <www.dolmen.com.mt>.* A large and popular, easygoing family hotel facing the sea, located midway between quiet Qawra and Buġibba with its bustling nightlife. Facilities include swimming pools, tennis, gym, and the Oracle Casino with a slot machine hall as well as the traditional gaming room. 380 rooms and 2 junior suites.

Gillieru Harbour €€€ *Church Square, St Paul's Bay SPB 01, tel: 2157 2720, fax: 2157 2745, <www.gillieru.com>.* Situated on the seafront next to a fishing harbour and the church square of St Paul's Bay, it is ideal for strolling to the restaurants and bars. Facilities include two restaurants, bar, pool, games room, watersports. 50 rooms.

Mellieha Bay €€€–€€€€ *Mellieha Bay, Ghadira SPB 10, tel: 2157 3841, fax: 2157 6399, <www.melliehabay.com>.* This large hotel faces Ghadira, the biggest sandy beach on Malta. Bus routes to Valetta or Ċirkewwa for the Gozo ferry pass directly outside. The hotel is popular with tour groups. Facilities include restaurant, four bars, indoor and outdoor swimming pools, tennis courts, watersports, garden and nightclub. 310 rooms.

Paradise Bay €€€–€€€€ *Ċirkewwa SPB 10, tel: 2157 3981, fax: 2152 1153, <www.paradise-bay.com>.* A large hotel on the western tip of Malta, overlooking the ferry dock for Gozo. There's a popular dive facility here, but no restaurants or bars around the hotel. Facilities include two restaurants, two bars, private beach, indoor and outdoor pools, tennis courts, shopping arcade. 217 rooms.

Selmun Palace €€€€ *Selmun, Mellieha SPB 10, tel: 2152 1040, fax: 2152 1159, <www.selmunpalacehotel.com>.* Situated on a hill, high above Mellieha Bay on the west of Malta, this hotel comprises an 18th-century castle with an extensive but sympathetic modern addition. Facilities include a gourmet restaurant in the castle's former chapel, restaurant, bar, indoor and outdoor swimming pools, game room, gym, private beach and tennis courts. 154 rooms, 6 suites in castle.

Suncrest €€€ *Qawra Coast Road, Qawra SPB 08, tel: 2157 7101, fax: 2157 5478, <www.suncresthotels.com>.* A large hotel overlooking the bay at Qawra within easy reach of lively Buġibba with its clubs, bars and nightlife. Facilities include six restaurants, four bars, disco, shopping arcade, indoor and outdoor swimming pools, garden, gym, sauna, squash court, tennis court and watersports. Good wheelchair access. 434 rooms.

Sunny Coast Resort €€€ *Qawra Bay SPB 1981, tel: 2157 2994, fax: 2157 6820, <www.sunnycoast.com.mt>*. Large family-oriented holiday hotel facing into bay. Pools, restaurants and kids' entertainment. A stroll away from the busy centre of Buġibba.

MDINA AND CENTRAL MALTA

Corinthia Palace €€€€€ *De Paule Avenue, Attard BZN 05, tel: 2144 0301, fax: 2146 5713, <www.corinthiahotels.com>*. A luxury resort hotel in the centre of the island, the Corinthia Palace, with its superb landscaped gardens, is the dowager of Malta's hotels. Guests can use beach and watersports facilities at the sister hotel, Corinthia San Gorġ in St Julians. 155 rooms.

Xara Palace €€€€€ *Misrah il-Kunsill, Mdina MDN 02, tel: 2145 0560, fax: 2145 2612, <www.xarapalace.com.mt>*. Beautiful small hotel located in the bastions of the medieval citadel. The rooms are furnished to the highest standards. A perfect place for a romantic getaway. Facilities include two restaurants, bar, sundeck. 17 suites.

COMINO

Comino €€€ *Island of Comino, SPB 10, tel: 2152 9821, fax: 2152 9826, <www.cominohotels.com>*. Comino island's only hotel. Facilities include two restaurants, pool, health club, tennis courts, games room, hairdresser. Closed end Oct–Easter. 95 rooms.

GOZO

Calypso €€€€ *Marsalforn, tel: 2156 2000, fax: 2156 2012, <www.hotelcalypsogozo.com>*. Long-established but refurbished in 2003, this hotel has a new image with upgraded rooms and facilities. It is ideal for families as it is only steps from the sea and the promenade. Restaurants, tennis and squash courts. 100 rooms.

Cornucopia €€€ *10 Gnien Imrik Street, Xagħra VCT 110, tel: 2155 6486, fax: 2155 2910*. Pretty hotel in the centre of the island, based on a converted farmhouse. Lots of atmosphere. Facilities include two swimming pools, restaurant, bar, games room, hair-dresser (also self-catering bungalows and converted farm houses). 50 rooms and suites.

The Grand €€€€ *Triq Sant Antnin, Għajnsielem GSM 104, tel: 2156 3840, fax: 2155 9744, <www.grandhotelmalta.com>.* An attractive hotel on hillside above the port of Mġarr with its fishing boats, ferries and fish restaurants. Many rooms with sea views, others overlook countryside. Jacuzzi and balconies. Restaurant and small roof-pool. 46 rooms.

Kempinski San Lawrenz & Spa €€€€€ *Triq ir-Rokon, San Lawrenz, GRB 104, tel: 2211 0000, fax: 2211 3746, <www.kempinskigozo. com>.* Located outside the tiny village of San Lawrenz and near the Inland Sea, this comfortable hotel has excellent facilities plus a Thalgo spa with marine algae therapy and an Ayurveda centre. Conference facilities, pools, restaurants and floodlit tennis. 106 rooms and suites.

San Andrea €€€ *Xatt ix-Klendi, Xlendi VCT 115, tel: 2156 5555, fax: 2156 5400, <www.hotelsanandrea.com>.* Small, simple hotel on the seafront with charming service. Simple restaurant. 28 rooms, some with sea views.

St Patrick's €€€ *Xatt ix-Xlendi, Xlendi VCT 115, tel: 2156 2951, fax: 2155 2951, <www.vjborg.com>.* Beautifully located on the harbour in the picturesque cove at Xlendi, this hotel takes design features from traditional buildings. Some rooms have windows and balconies overlooking the inner courtyard, others have views over the bay. Facilities include restaurant, bar, splash pool, whirlpool. 45 rooms.

Ta' Ċenċ €€€€ *Sannat VTC 112, tel: 2155 6819, fax: 2155 8199, <www.vjborg.com>.* In a secluded country location but with a private beach, Ta' Ċenċ is probably the best hotel in the islands. Facilities include a restaurant, bar, two swimming pools, excellent health spa, tennis courts and whirlpool. Be sure to explore the nearby dolmen and other ancient remains. 83 rooms and suites.

Recommended Restaurants

Both Malta and Gozo have a wide variety of restaurants to choose from, some expensive, some definitely not so – especially if you compare their prices with similar establishments in the rest of western Europe. Fish can be costly. A few restaurants serve a selection of traditional Maltese dishes. Also on offer are well-known, international brand, fast-food outlets and the islands' own pizza and pasta establishments.

At the top end of the scale, where standards remain consistently high, there are Rubino and Ambrosia in Valletta, La Dolce Vita or San Giuliano at St Julian's, Lord Nelson at Mosta or, in Gozo, il-Panzier in Victoria and it-Tmum at Xlendi and at Victoria. On a tighter budget there is an ample selection; many of the most popular are listed here. As a general rule, if a restaurant is busy, it is good value.

All restaurants are air-conditioned and many also have open-air terraces or gardens that are used in the summer months. A new law came into force in 2004 which bans smoking in places providing a service to the public. So all restaurants now are officially designated smoke-free unless in a garden or terrace.

The following symbols give you an idea of the approximate price of a three-course dinner with wine per person:

€€€€	over 35 euros
€€€	22–35 euros
€€	12–22 euros
€	below 12 euros

MALTA

VALLETTA

Ambrosia €€€€ *137 Archbishop's Street, tel: 2122 5923.* Located in a street alongside the Palace, this is an excellent restaurant with a menu that changes daily. Good starters, delicious main courses, all characterised by a seasonal Mediterranean slant. A fine wine list complements the food. Booking essential.

Blue Room €€€€ *58 Republic Street, tel: 2123 8014*. Chinese restaurant close to the Palace with charming staff and a reputation for serving the best of Cantonese dishes. Popular, so booking is recommended. Closed Mon. Wheelchair access.

Castille Hotel €€€ *Castille Square, tel: 2124 3677*. At night, when the lights come on, the hotel's roof restaurant enjoys fine views of the Grand Harbour and Malta. Menu of simple international dishes.

Fumia €€€ *Old Bakery Street, tel: 2131 7053*. Below the Manoel Theatre, this Italian restaurant with excellent pasta and meat dishes is a favourite with theatregoers and visiting international singers and musicians who crowd there after performances. Booking recommended. Entrance by steep staircase.

Giannini €€€€ *St Michael's Bastion (off Windmill Street), tel: 2123 7121*. In a patrician house overlooking Marsamxett Harbour, with Manoel Island and Sliema across the bay. Ground-floor bar, and elevator to the top-floor restaurant with panoramic views. There is a small terrace with four tables. Pasta, fish and roasts, the speciality of the Italian chef, are highly rated. Booking essential for dinner Fri and Sat. Wheelchair access.

Malata €€€€ *Palace Square, tel: 2123 3967*. With an entrance on the square facing the Palace, the restaurant has an excellent menu that appeals to politicians (Parliament is across the road) and businessmen. Live jazz two nights a week.

Da Pippo €€€ *136 Melita Street, tel: 2124 8029*. Lunch only, but worth a visit for the generous portions of good, wholesome food cooked according to the chef's preference for Maltese dishes. Very popular so booking is essential.

Rubino €€€€ *54 Old Bakery Street, tel: 2122 4656*. Rated among the best in Malta, with consistently high standards. Good atmosphere, good food, good crowd. Menu changes daily but includes Maltese as well as Mediterranean dishes. Lunch Mon–Sat, dinner Tues and Thur. Book.

SLIEMA

Barracuda €€€€ *195 Main Street, tel: 2133 1817.* Overlooking Balluta Bay and the sea, a pretty restaurant that is sometimes considered pricey, but nevertheless recommended by regulars. Fresh fish a speciality. Book. Wheelchair access.

Can Thai €€€ *Fortina Spa Resort, Tigne Sea Front, tel: 2346 0000.* One of the hotel's popular themed restaurants set around an outdoor pool. Chinese and Thai dishes. Open daily.

Galeone €€€ *35 Tigne Sea Front, tel: 2131 6420.* A casual neighbourhood restaurant with the owner as chef. His recommendations are worth following. Good pasta, fish, steaks.

Piccolo Padre €€€ *195 Main Street, tel: 2134 4875.* A delightful pizzeria beneath the Barracuda restaurant (see above). Great pizza and pasta in informal setting; popular with families and children. Maltese and Gozitan ingredients add extra interest to some dishes. A number of tables overlook the bay. No bookings taken. Queueing at weekends. Take-away available.

Ta'Kris €€ *80 Fawwara Lane, Bisazza Street, tel: 2133 7367.* Located in a quiet alley, this is an inexpensive haunt popular with the locals. The menu is varied, with most dishes cooked in the flavoursome Maltese manner. Casual, with friendly service. At weekends, booking is essential.

TGI Fridays €€€ *Il-Fortizza, Tower Road, tel: 2133 6908.* This chain of restaurants is known for its American-style burgers, steaks and finger food, but none of their other outlets is as imposing as this one, which is housed in a 17th-century fort on the Sliema promenade. Informal atmosphere with loud music. Open daily. Wheelchair access.

Vino Veritas €€€ *59 Sir Adrian Dingli Street, tel: 2132 4273.* Amiable trattoria with relaxed atmosphere. Trattoria-style cooking. Open Tues–Sat. Wheelchair access.

ST JULIANS AND PACEVILLE

Bottega del Vino €€€ *at the Hilton Malta, Portomaso, tel: 2133 6201.* In a gracious setting, this is one of the Hilton's five restaurants. The menu of simple Maltese and Italian dishes includes rabbit and Maltese sausages. Open daily.

Bouzouki €€€ *135 Spinola Road, St Julians, tel: 2131 7127.* Greek taverna in up-market surroundings with open-air terrace on the quay. Salads, souvlaki, slow-cooked stews. Open daily.

Caffè Rafael €€€ *Spinola Road, St Julians Bay, tel: 2131 9988.* Large, pretty, terraced café under the same management as San Giuliano restaurant (see below). Good-value café food in pleasant location. Wheelchair access.

La Dolce Vita €€€€ *159 St George's Road, tel: 2133 7806.* Always busy with a mainly young crowd. There are wonderful views across the bay. The specialities are pasta and fish. Open daily. Book for best tables. Wheelchair access.

Peppino's €€€ *30 St George's Road, tel: 2137 3200.* Buzzing bar on the ground floor and popular restaurant on the upper floors, favoured by locals looking for light wines and an inexpensive lunch. The restaurant, which serves Italian food and fresh fish, also has a roof terrace. Crowded at weekends.

Saddles €€€ *132 Main Street, tel: 2133 9993.* Situated at the hub of St Julians Bay, Saddles is a bar that attracts the beer, wine and hamburger set. Flashy cars and motorbikes keep the regulars in constant motion.

San Giuliano €€€€€ *Spinola Road, tel: 2133 2000.* If you are a visiting movie star shooting a film in Malta, this is where you are seen and given star treatment. Sometimes considered the smartest meeting place. Good-looking Italian restaurant with a view over St Julians waterfront. The menu features many fish and seafood dishes. Booking recommended.

Tana del Lupo €€€€ *58 Triq il-Wilga, Paceville, tel: 2135 3294*. Bustling and often hectic Sicilian restaurant that is always crowded. Excellent pasta dishes, but specialities are fish and seafood. Pavement tables outside in summer months. Booking advisable.

Terrazza €€€ *Spinola Waterfront, St Julians, tel: 2138 4939*. The terrace restaurant is perched above boathouses and has splendid views over the bay. Young crowd, friendly service. Menu interesting and changes often. Look for pasta and meat specialities.

MELLIEĦA

The Arches €€€€€ *113 Main Street, tel: 2152 3460*. In central Mellieha, a large and brightly lit, colourful place with bustling service and large portions. Roof open in summer. Wide international menu. Booking advisable. Wheelchair access.

Giuseppi's €€€ *25 St Helen's Street, tel: 2157 4882*. On two floors, Giuseppi's is considered a fine example of a truly Maltese restaurant, both in decor and in cooking. High standards come from an imaginative chef. Menu changes daily and is seasonal. Very popular so booking advised.

MARSASCALA

Grabiel €€€€€ *Marsascala Bay, tel: 2168 4194*. Highly rated family-run fish restaurant that has built up a serious local following of diners who come here for the catches of the day, the octopus stew and, when in season, the *pasta rizzi* (spaghetti with sea urchins). The fish is sold by weight for some of the dishes. Crowded and noisy. Booking essential. Open lunch and dinner daily. Wheelchair access and facilities.

La Favorita €€€ *Gardiel Street, tel: 2163 4113*. On the narrow road heading to St Thomas's Bay, this is an informal, family restaurant with a reputation for its consistently high standard of fish, which is unpretentiously served. Crowded and noisy at weekends, when booking imperative. Open daily. Wheelchair access.

MARSAXLOKK

Ir-Rizzu €€€ *89 The Waterfront, tel: 2165 1569*. Friendly, family-run waterfront restaurant offering a range of dishes alongside its fresh fish specialities that are so popular with regular customers. Booking is essential. Open daily. Wheelchair access.

Is-Sajjied €€€ *The Waterfront, tel: 2165 2549*. On the jetty, with charm and character. Not surprisingly, fish is the speciality here, but there are also pasta dishes and traditional soups on offer, along with a selection of vegetarian and meat dishes. Open terrace in the summer has delightful views. Open daily. Wheelchair access.

MDINA

Bacchus €€€€ *1 Inguanez Street, tel: 2145 4981*. Located in the bastion walls of the city, with entrance down a narrow side street. Large and popular, specialising in Maltese, French and Italian cooking. A good place for parties. Open daily.

Medina €€€€ *7 Holy Cross Street, tel: 2145 4004*. A pretty courtyard restaurant, complete with tall oleander tree. A romantic setting. International cooking with British overtones. Wheelchair access.

De Mondian €€€€€ *Xara Palace Hotel, tel: 2145 0560*. This is the roof-top restaurant of the gracious hotel perched on the bastion walls. Fine views of the countryside. Dinner only. The international menu and wines reflect the hotel's sense of status and occasion.

Trattoria AD1530 €€€ *Xara Palace Hotel, tel: 2145 0560*. Simple trattoria with tables in the piazza outside the 5-star hotel. Pasta, pizza and simple Italian dishes. Lunch and dinner. A meeting place.

MOSTA

Lord Nelson €€€€ *278 Main Street, Mosta, tel: 2143 2590*. Once a village corner bar, the Lord Nelson is now an attractive restaurant renowned for consistently good cooking and a menu unlike any other on the islands. Both popular and fashionable. Booking essential. Wheelchair access downstairs.

QAWRA

Gran Laguna €€€€ *Triq il-Qala, tel: 2157 1146*. Hard to find, but with Sicilian cooking of high quality. Known for its pasta and fresh fish as well as its Italian clientele. Book in summer months.

Savini €€€€€ *Qawra Road, tel: 2157 6927*. Located in a converted old farmhouse on the outskirts of Buġibba, Savini has open-air terraces and a garden for dining in the summer months. Rich Italian cooking served graciously. Regarded by some as one of the island's top restaurants.

RABAT

Grapes €€€ *1 Catacombs Street, tel: 2145 0483*. Small, cosy restaurant, close to the catacombs. Serves Maltese dishes and Maltese wine. Open Mon–Sat.

Gusmana Navarra €€€ *28 St Paul's Street, tel: 2145 0638*. Opposite St Paul's Church in an old house. Café on ground floor serves snacks; restaurant on floor above serves meat and fish dishes. Open Mon–Sat.

Il Veduta €€€ *Saqqija Square, tel: 2145 4666*. Simple pizza and pasta restaurant hidden behind Mdina Gate car park. Wonderful view from its open terrace in summer. Casual atmosphere. Popular and crowded. Open daily. Wheelchair access.

ST PAUL'S BAY

Gillieru €€€€€ *Church Street, tel: 2157 3480*. Jutting out into the bay – with an open terrace that is crowded in summer – this long-established fish restaurant is unsophisticated and friendly. Regulars praise the grilled fish, but there are also meat dishes, with traditional Maltese fare such as rabbit stew. Open daily. Wheelchair access.

Da Rosi €€€ *45 Church Street, tel: 2157 1411*. Pretty but small, a friendly family-run restaurant with a fine menu of international dishes. Booking essential at weekends.

GOZO

GĦARB

Jeffrey's €€€€ *10 Triq il-Għarb, tel: 2156 1006*. Next door to Gozo Glass, outside Għarb. Excellent little trattoria serving only seasonal dishes. Courtyard dining in summer. Dinner only. Closed Sun and winter until about Easter. Booking recommended. Wheelchair access.

Salvina's €€€€ *21 Frenc tal-Għarb, tel: 2155 2505*. Pretty little restaurant in village house on a quaint, narrow village street. There's a small courtyard for alfresco dining. Local and international cuisine. Closed Thur.

MARSALFORN

Il-Kartell €€€€ *Marina Street, tel: 2155 6918*. Housed in three connected former boathouses, this popular restaurant has tables outside on the water's edge of the harbour, weather permitting. Friendly atmosphere, good fish and local dishes as well as pasta and pizzas. Wheelchair access. Closed January and Wed lunch

Ta' Frenc €€€€€ *Triq Għajn Damma, off Marsalforn Road, tel: 2155 3888*. Wide range of traditional Maltese and international cuisine, and children's dishes, elegantly presented in a stylishly converted 14th-century farmhouse. Rustic interior with vaulted ceilings, and beautiful garden for alfresco dining. Open daily. Wheelchair access and facilities.

Otter's €€€ *Triq Santa Marija, tel: 2156 2473*. Casual café perched on ledge above the sea and waterpolo pitch. Simple, good-value café food served with welcoming charm. Popular. Wheelchair access and facilities. The owners, brothers, also run three Café Jubilees – one in Victoria *(see page 140)* and two in Malta (Valletta and Gżira).

MĠARR

Il-Kcina tal-Barrakka €€€ *28 Triq Manuel de Vilhena, tel: 2155 6543.* Known to all as Sammy's, after the proprietor. Like its neighbour Manoel's (see above) this is where the crowd comes to dine casually on fresh pasta and fish. Many diners come from Malta, as it is within walking distance of the ferry. Small, with imaginative menu. Closed Nov–May. Booking essential. Wheelchair access.

Manoel's €€€ *27 Triq Manoel de Vilhena, tel: 2156 3588.* Dinner only. Dress: anything goes. Crowded and popular, with good pasta and fish at reasonable prices (unless an expensive foreign wine is selected). A fine view of colourful fishing boats in the harbour. Wheelchair access.

SANNAT

Il-Carrubo €€€€€ *Ta' Ċenċ Hotel, tel: 2155 6819.* Gourmet restaurant serving Italian and Gozitan dishes. Dine under the carob tree in the summer months, with live music. Open daily. Wheelchair access.

VICTORIA

Café Jubilee €€ *8 Independence Square (It-Tokk), tel: 2155 8921.* Informal café dressed up to represent a French bistro c.1920. Wide range of snacks. Popular bar at weekends so very crowded. Tables also on the square.

Il-Panzier €€€€€ *Triq il-Karita, tel: 2155 9979.* Gozo's most elegant restaurant is hidden discreetly in a winding medieval street off It-Tokk. The limited menu is offset by the superior Italian cuisine. Courtyard dining. Dinner only. Closed Mon.

It-Tmun €€€€ *Europe Street, tel: 2156 6667.* Attractive busy restaurant that is an extension of It-Tmun in Xlendi. A young crowd gathers here. The wide menu has a selection of dishes that are cooked in the Maltese manner. Seasonal fresh fish and seafood. Dinner only. Book at weekends.

Ta' Riccardo € *4 Triq il-Fosos, in the Citadel, tel: 2155 5953*. A wine barrel topped with fresh bread and tomatoes signals the door into one of the oldest houses in the Citadel. Traditional Gozitan snacks make for light, cold lunches. The wine is made on the premises. This is an excellent, easy stop when exploring the walled city. Souvenirs, including honey and other Gozitan produce, are also available here.

XAGĦRA

Gesther €€€ *8 September Avenue, tel: 2155 6621*. A very, very casual and cramped space, but this is authentic local food lovingly prepared with much of the produce from their own fields. Good value for bigger appetites. Lunch only. Closed Sun.

Oleander €€€€ *10 Victory Square, tel: 2155 7230*. With some tables outside in the main square, the Oleander is known for its excellent local dishes, fish and steaks. Inside can be noisy as it is popular. Book. Wheelchair access.

XLENDI

Il Terrazzo €€€ *St Simon Street, tel: 2156 2992*. Pretty restaurant on the hillside, with panoramic views over the bay from the dining terrace. The menu includes a range of pasta dishes and various fresh fish specialities, as well as meat dishes. Open daily.

It-Tmun €€€€€ *3 Trejqet il-Madonna tal-Karmnu, tel: 2155 1571*. Intimate little restaurant considered by many to be the finest in Gozo. Booking is therefore essential. Excellent pasta and fish. Tables outside in summer months. Open daily.

Paradise €€€ *Trejqet il-Madonna tal-Karmnu, tel: 2155 6878*. Fondly known by aficionados as the Elvis Presley Memorial Bar because memorabilia of 'the King' decorates the walls. Basic comfort but excellent simple cooking, including fresh fish and jumbo prawns. Exceptionally good value. Tables outside in the summer. Wheelchair access.

INDEX

Berlitz pocket guide

Malta

Sixth Edition 2008
Written by Lindsay Bennett
Updated by Geoffrey Aquilina Ross
Principal photographer: Pete Bennett
Series Editor: Tony Halliday

Photography credits
Pete Bennett 1, 9, 12, 13, 14, 16, 20, 24, 26, 29, 31, 32, 34, 37, 38, 41, 42, 43, 44, 45, 49, 50, 51, 52, 57, 59, 60, 61, 62, 67, 68, 69, 70, 72, 73, 75, 79, 80, 82, 83, 88, 90, 91, 93, 97, 98; Glyn Genin 6, 11, 47, 53, 54, 56, 58, 65, 76, 77, 85, 86, 94; Sovereign Order of St John 18, 19

Cover picture: Jaubert Bernard/Alamy

Printed in Singapore by Insight Print Services (Pte) Ltd, 38 Joo Koon Road, Singapore 628990. Tel: (65) 6865-1600. Fax: (65) 6861-6438

Berlitz Trademark Reg. U.S. Patent Office and other countries. Marca Registrada

Every effort has been made to provide accurate information in this publication, but changes are inevitable. The publisher cannot be responsible for any resulting loss, inconvenience or injury.

Contact us

At Berlitz we strive to keep our guides as accurate and up to date as possible, but if you find anything that has changed, or if you have any suggestions on ways to improve this guide, then we would be delighted to hear from you.

Berlitz Publishing, PO Box 7910, London SE1 1WE, England.
fax: (44) 20 7403 0290
email: berlitz@apaguide.co.uk
www.berlitzpublishing.com